Rethinking Creative Writing
in Higher Education

Programs and practices that work

Stephanie M. Vanderslice, M.F.A., Ph.D.

Imprint Information and Credits

ISBN: 978-1-907076-31-2 (paperback)
ISBN: 978-1-907076-13-8 (hardback)

Published under the Creative Writing Studies imprint by
The Professional and Higher Partnership Ltd
Registered office: Mill House, 21 High Street, Wicken,
Ely, Cambs, CB7 5XR, UK

Imprint website: creativewritingstudies.wordpress.com
Company website: www.professionalandhigher.com

First published 2011
© Stephanie Vanderslice
The right of Stephanie Vanderslice to be identified as the author
of this Work has been asserted by her in accordance with the
Copyright, Designs and Patents Act 1988.

Credits
Abstract: Anthony Haynes
Copy-editing: Karen Haynes
Design and typesetting: Benn Linfield (www.bennlinfield.com)
E-book conversion: FirstyWork (www.firstywork.com)
Index: Christina Garbutt
Proofreading: Richard Kitchen
Printing: Printondemandworldwide
   (www.printondemandworldwide.com)

Disclaimer

Series Information

Rethinking Creative Writing in Higher Education forms the first title in the international series, Creative Writing Studies. The series comprises titles on creative writing designed for use – by scholars, students, and teachers – in higher education settings.

Further titles commissioned for the series include:
Researching Creative Writing by Jen Webb
Teaching Creative Writing, edited by Elaine Walker
Creative Writing, edited by Amal Chatterjee

*This book is dedicated to
the writers of the future.*

Table of Contents

Abstract

Creative writing as a discipline is a victim of its own success. The discipline needs now to demythogize and revitalize itself. Undergraduate and graduate programs need to be further differentiated. Programs over-reliant on the traditional creative writing workshop, with its focus on craft and on building community, are ill equipped to prepare students for the new realities of the creative economy. Programs need not only to improve the workshop experience of students, but also employ a more diverse, outward-looking, outcomes-oriented pedagogy and to make a more direct contribution to the development of a literate society. Much can be learnt from good practice – including distinctive and visionary programs – developed on both sides of the Atlantic and in Australia.

KEY TERMS
creative writing; literacy; pedagogy; programs; reflective; reform; teaching; visionary; workshop

Foreword

This is a brave, serious, passionate and entertaining book. It is the book the author (as she puts it) "had to write;" a book, incidentally, that she is probably uniquely qualified to write, the result of some twenty years experience and enquiry. This book is personal, while also taking on big public questions of community, literacy, and the uses of writing.

Stephanie Vanderslice relentlessly confronts the central issues surrounding the teaching of Creative Writing as an academic discipline – issues that some creative writing tutors might frankly prefer to ignore. You see, the author is not prepared to compromise, not prepared to let a nod or a wink suffice, nor to paper over inconsistencies, nor to accept sloppy thinking, nor to tolerate the scam of programmes and teachers taking money while lacking conviction or commitment.

In short, she will not let us lie, she will not allow us to be complacent or negligent. She demands to know what we are teaching our students, and why; she digs through the habit and mysticism to lay bare the pedagogies (or lack of them) beneath; she gives the workshop a thorough going over; she insists on a rich version and vision of the "writing life"; on a conception beyond craft, that includes a vibrant creativity, but also refuses to have any truck with mystery or miracle in the explanation of process or tuition.

Also (and this is important) she knows her stuff. She doesn't rely on anecdote or bar room tattle. She's done the miles across the academic Creative Writing world, and she understands it inside out.

For me as a Creative Writing programme leader, reading this book is rather like a hotelier experiencing a visit from an enthusiastic, deeply expert, boundlessly energetic, unfailingly helpful, but always observant – painfully observant – Public Health Inspector, who breezes through my staff rooms and classrooms pointing out unexplored corners, unbrushed assumptions, misconceptions, fudges and dusty window ledges; who will not for a moment allow complacency or negligence; but above all who does it all with a sweet and humorous style that leaves me feeling cleansed and inspired about my self, my subject and my students.

If you care about Creative Writing, I recommend this book to you wholeheartedly.

STEVE MAY
Head of the Creative Writing Department
Bath Spa University
United Kingdom

Chapter One

Creative Writing in Higher Education: Reflection, Innovation, Accountability

"At a time when the humanities in general are at risk and under siege, the tendency is to circle the wagons and stridently define the integrity of our departments ... however, we might also choose to look outward ... for ways in which our writing can meet, engage and challenge mass culture."

(Mike Chasar, *Remembering Paul Engle*)

Why this book?

Because it's time. Time to unlock the potential creative writing programs have to revitalize writing in higher education. Time to uncircle the wagons that have defended so many of them, for so long, from reflection, innovation and accountability.

Creative writing programs have been fixtures on the academic landscape since the MFA (Master of Fine Arts) program that started them all was founded at the University of Iowa in 1941. Besides providing a steady source of writing talent to the American literary scene, a phenomenon luminously documented in Mark McGurl's history, *The Program Era: Postwar Fiction and the Rise of Creative Writing*, the MFA in writing at Iowa had an important ripple effect as its graduates fanned out across the country to found programs of their own. By 1967 there were 13 programs, a critical number that resulted in R.V. Cassill's founding of the Associated Writing Programs (now called The Association of Writers and Writing Programs, or AWP) that year. Creative writing had officially "arrived" on college campuses and by all indication was there to stay.

Indeed, the decades of the late twentieth century were heady times for creative writing, as writers flexed their muscles and discovered the joys and challenges to be had in creating communities that nurtured the next Philip Roths and Flannery O'Connors. Community is the operative word here, for sometimes the intensity and distinctiveness of creative writing in the academic setting, within a larger western culture where artistic endeavors exist at the fringes of society at best, can be so heady as to convince its members that community is *enough*. Even today, McGurl points out that creative writing programs are privileged as "occasions for enabling intimacy" and community, harking all the way back to the time when Paul Engle, the University of Iowa Writing Program's visionary leader, built his "international community of the imagination" (2009, p. 173).

There is nothing wrong with this sense of community; in fact the buffer it provides between the artist and the rest of the world is absolutely critical to any writing program. When I was a young MFA student at George Mason University, our professor, novelist Richard Bausch, used to remind us to cherish our community of writers above all else because once we passed through our classroom doors, we would find ourselves back in a world where words and literature did not matter to most people, at least not the way they did to us. He was right – the community I found there supported and accelerated my development as a writer. But personal history aside, communities like mine at George Mason, nurtured by the resident writers who teach in them, now flourish at hundreds of graduate creative writing programs across the country. Fifty-plus years after the University of Iowa birthed the first campus American literary salon, AWP records 336 graduate programs and 313 undergraduate creative writing programs and counting dotting our vast landscape (2009), while the UK counts 130 graduate and over 200 undergraduate programs (National Association of Writers in Education (NAWE) 2010), and Australia and New Zealand 21 graduate and 17 undergraduate programs (Australasian Association of Writing Programs (AAWP) 2010). Meanwhile, the landscape itself has changed dramatically. An ever more competitive, monolithic publishing industry, a dwindling public readership (in the strictest literary sense) and ever evolving new media are just some of the faces of the new "normal," with which thousands of aspiring writers must contend. Given these realities, all of which require a host of new knowledge and skills from the aspiring writer that a general creative writing workshop cannot possibly contain, the undisputed intensity of the writing communities created by these programs is simply no longer enough. Instead, this community must be *built upon* with a curriculum that consciously empowers students to learn new ways of thriving as writers as publishing evolves, to find their footing in a world where mid-list authors are fast becoming an endangered species while those who can provide creative content for digital media and the web take their place.

Beyond community
In a sense, creative writing in academia is a victim of its own success. Seven decades after the first university writing program was founded, the rise in demand for creative writing courses in higher education continues unabated.

The steady growth of MAs and MFAs post-Iowa led to a corresponding growth in undergraduate majors and courses, demonstrating that when it comes to creative writing programs in higher education, "if you build them, they will come," especially when building these programs is far less expensive than, say, outfitting a Physics graduate program with millions of dollars of lab equipment. As McGurl points out, even the lauded star writer can be had for less than a "particle accelerator," (2009, p. 407) and the star writer is likely to attract far more attention. Such rapid growth can – and did – lead to many hastily-constructed programs that served the cash cow they represented rather than the hopeful writers who populated them. After all, as many of these programs noted, and AWP Executive Director D.W. Fenza concurred in "Creative Writing and Its Discontents," "no advanced degree necessarily secures jobs for artists" (2001). Unfortunately, such sentiments also absolved these programs of any responsibility toward providing more thoughtful, outcomes-oriented curricula.

A few sentences later, in the same essay, Fenza notes that "study in the arts is applicable to many types of employment outside academe." Perhaps having it "both ways," that is, claiming not to prepare creative writing graduate students for anything while at the same time asserting such programs prepared them for everything, was possible in the early days when the idea of creative writing on campus was relatively new. No longer. As Fenza points out, writing in higher education has been criticized many times, by many cultural critics, criticisms perhaps most aptly summarized by Mark McGurl when he describes a public perception of the postgraduate writing degree as a "costly extension of [the] liberal education … a prolongation of the 'college experience,' an all-too-brief period when the student is validated as a creative person and given temporary cover, by virtue of his student status, from the classic complaint of middle-class parents that their would-be artist children are being frivolous" (2009, p. 17).

Even as a critic of the status quo, it is hard for me, as a writing teacher and MFA graduate, to read such a casually dismissive description without wincing. Yet in the face of these charges I maintain, again and again, it *doesn't* have to be that way. The landscape can and must change. Yes, engaged, responsive programs are growing in number; you will learn about them in these pages. But they are still in the minority. Yes, as Fenza notes, an increasingly competitive market means that many of the writers who gain employment in these programs are responsible, dedicated teachers with the futures of their graduates at heart. But at the same time, as Edward Delaney describes as late as 2007 in an interview on these programs in *The Atlantic* fiction supplement, "there are still professors at some schools who barely seem to show up." Moreover, there are also professors who believe that showing up for a vigorous three-hour workshop and an hour at the bar afterward is enough.

So what does this kind of change look like? It is – and should be – different at different schools, but it boils down to what my colleague at Bath Spa University, Mimi Thebo, describes as "responsible creative writing teaching" (Bath Spa, you'll discover as you continue in this book, is a model for such teaching). It means that former students won't graduate from expensive MFA programs, racking up a mountain of debt, only to return to me desperate for career counseling and painfully naïve about what they need to compete for the most basic teaching job or to find a foothold in the creative economy.

It also means that the undergraduate creative writing program bears perhaps even more responsibility for a well-considered curriculum, one based less on the ubiquitous workshop that dominates graduate programs. As many field leaders admit, Fenza among them, undergraduate creative writing professors have often struggled in a vacuum (that being the absence of courses in creative writing pedagogy) to retrofit a graduate curriculum that doesn't really match their students, for reasons we will fully explore in the next chapter.

In fact, undergraduate professors and programs must fully recognize their potential to create degree programs featuring pedagogies, practices, indeed syllabi, tailored just for them, with less emphasis on the traditional workshop that evolved for graduate students and more on the types of coursework that will help them sustain writing lives after they graduate, whether they pursue an MFA, follow their love of writing into a corresponding career or continue, like Marianne Moore, T.S. Eliot and, more recently, Ted Kooser and Michael Cunningham, to write outside their "day" jobs. With the runaway growth of new media and the content it requires, and the rise of creative industry in general, now could hardly be a better time to steward such a curriculum, one poised to give students every advantage in the creative economy. Finally, in light of current exigencies in the publishing industry, shrinking publication opportunities for the first-time or mid-list author, the current explosion of MFA degrees and the resultant tidal wave of submissions to even the littlest of little magazines, as well as ever-shrinking employment opportunities in academia, it is no longer ethical for *graduate* program leaders to throw up their hands at the admitted crapshoot that any career in the arts can be and continue to promulgate programs dominated by workshops that do little to prepare students for life outside the ivory tower. Instead, it is the responsibility of these leaders to examine the state of the field and determine what can be done to transform a system that has chugged amiably along for the last half-century into a sleeker model more suited to functioning – and helping its students to function – in the twenty-first. The first step in this transformation? Creative writing programs in higher education must see themselves as accountable to their constituencies, rather than using the uncertainty of arts careers as a smokescreen. They must ask: how is the literary scene changing for our students? How can we better prepare them to enter it? What courses do we need to add to our curriculum? What content do we need to add to the courses we already teach? Certainly, no program can incorporate *all* of these changes. But all programs can re-examine their curricula with regard to where they can best focus their energies (new media? editing and publishing? book arts?) in order to best prepare their students for the new order.

What basis do I have to call for this reappraisal and remaking of creative writing in higher education, to declare that a change is not only possible but necessary? For one thing, besides cutting my teeth on one of these programs and since then becoming familiar, via study and travel, with many, many others, I have made the mechanisms of the creative writing classroom and the exploration of creative writing culture the central focus of my career.

This perspective has brought me in close contact with a number of like-minded individuals in the creative writing community – in fact, a number that has reached critical mass – who also recognize the need for reform, for transformation within the ranks. Individuals like the late Wendy Bishop and Katharine Haake who as early as the 2003 AWP conference called for a centralized depository of creative writing theory and pedagogy so that the right hand would not only know what the left hand was doing, but also what had already been accomplished and what remained to be done. A prolific poet and writing scholar, Wendy Bishop was perhaps the first American writer to crack open the mystique of the creative writing classroom and train a magnifying glass on it in the same way she examined her teaching in the composition classroom, an examination that resulted in countless articles and books on the teaching of creative writing, an oeuvre that literally gave birth to the discipline in America.

Walking alongside these pioneers today are teacher/ writers like Tim Mayers, Anna Leahy, Mary Ann Cain, Patrick Bizarro, and many others who contributed to *Can It Really Be Taught?: Resisting Lore in Creative Writing Pedagogy*, the collection edited by Kelly Ritter and myself designed to leapfrog creative writing beyond the folklore and myth that has traditionally bound the field, who have all pushed for changes in the status quo. Despite the protestations of writers like Timothy Houghton (2006, p. 198), who insist that creative writers in academia cannot attend to both their own work and to the programmatic and pedagogic needs of their students, I have seen that such combined purposes are more than possible, their yield far more rich for all parties involved than what will be here characterized as creative writing "old school." Examples of these combined purposes, of creative writing "new school," are rarer than they should be; however, such rarity is the driving force of this book. *Rethinking Creative Writing* will feature them in detail with the intention of inspiring, if not prodding, others who might deem my recommendations too idealistic.

For the past several years I have studied the programs and pedagogies of creative writing in postsecondary education in the United Kingdom, a pursuit that has further revealed the potential of postsecondary creative writing. Once my eyes were opened, moreover, I began to look more closely at the many writing programs in the US that were also in the vanguard. Finally, my international work has brought me in close contact with teachers and writers representing the rich campus creative writing scenes in Australia. This book will bring together best practice from all of them to inspire us to revisit our work, to rethink creative writing in higher education.

What this book is not

In his book about social justice and liberation theology, *Liberating Jonah: Forming an Ethics of Reconciliation*, Miguel de la Torre (2007) takes a swipe at academics who write prolifically about flaws in the social order but do precious little to change them. Although I admire the book and de la Torre's passion, on this point I disagree. Academics *must* write prodigiously about flaws in any system, *especially their own*, dissecting them with a scalpel for all the world, in order to underscore the need for change. Many of the scholars I have already mentioned have done this and while there is always room for new scholarship, I am quite sure that the case has already been made for a more reflective theory- and practice-based Creative Writing Studies (Mayers 2009) discipline that will undergird the teaching of creative writing in higher education. Using that work as a foundation, this book will provide concrete next actions that will usher in this transformation: creative writing programs dedicated to helping their constituencies, their students, meet the challenges of the present and the future.

From community to responsibility

At this point, I suspect my readers fall into two categories: those who agree that creative writing programs in higher education could certainly do with more than a little tweaking and those who have begun to make a list of reasons why creative writing in higher education ain't broke, so why fix it when our time could be more efficiently spent writing works of fiction, poetry, creative nonfiction and so forth, the *real* work of our field. In either case, I invite you to read on, although, perhaps in the latter case I ask you to take a deep breath, put down your red pen and see what I have to say.

As I alluded to earlier, considered, thoughtful, even vanguard programs are beginning to dot the landscape. In fact, many of them have sprung up in the United Kingdom and Australia, where much exciting work is being done overall in postsecondary creative writing theory, education and curriculum. I don't mean to privilege the practices of programs in these countries over those in the US. Let me repeat, it was innovations abroad that opened my eyes to those occurring in vanguard programs on our own soil. I strongly advocate more cross-fertilization, however, between and among programs in the anglophile world (and in the future, beyond it).

Before we go on, however, a brief summary of the cultural, political and educational context of programmatic differences in the UK is in order if we are to understand what they have to show those of us who want creative writing in higher education to not only survive, but thrive. When Malcolm Bradbury transplanted the idea of the graduate creative writing workshop to the United Kingdom in the late 1960s, specifically to the University of East Anglia (where he and Angus Wilson would later found the first MA program in Creative Writing in 1970) the seeds of the "workshop" remained the same. The terroir was vastly different, however, and necessarily resulted in vastly different crops emerging in both undergraduate and postgraduate programs over the next thirty years. An important soil variation, tied more closely to the undergraduate program in the UK, relates to the fact that many of these programs in the UK emerged in the last ten to fifteen years in what can effectively be described as "Post-Dearing Report" Britain. A government-commissioned document published in 1997 by the National Committee of Inquiry into Higher Education, the Dearing Report, named for its head, Lord Ron Dearing, thoroughly examined higher education in the UK and, in referencing a growing trend in outcomes-based education in that country (and on the continent as well), recommended that all programs in higher education clearly demonstrate their learning outcomes, especially with regard to skills that could be transferred beyond the ivory tower (obviously this is a brief summary; the report itself is 1,700 pages long).

Education at all levels in the United Kingdom is much more centrally regulated than that in the United States, especially higher education, which in the US is loosely regulated if at all. The Quality Assurance Agency for Higher Education (QAAHE), for example, is a UK regulating agency that enforced these recommendations by auditing their implementation at universities and colleges. Because so many UK creative writing programs were founded or necessarily revised during the post-Dearing era, their curricula and programs of study reveal concrete connections to intended learning outcomes, learning outcomes that emerged from a great deal of reflection and interrogation on the teaching of a subject that many in the US continue to resist interrogating on the grounds that creative writing cannot be taught – even as they make their livelihoods by teaching it.

Graduate programs in the UK were likewise accountable to the exigencies of the Dearing report, but they also served an even more demanding god: their own students and, by extension, their students' success. Such programs are comparatively expensive and rarely funded by scholarships (bursaries) or the teaching assistantships so common in the US. Consequently, students in these programs, unless they are independently wealthy, must sacrifice in any number of ways to attend them. Not surprisingly, they are frugal and discriminating with their tuition dollars. In order to compete for the best students, even mid-list programs must demonstrate that their faculty are not only well published but that they are *dedicated* to the ultimate publishing success of their students. As a result, rather than surrender to the idea that they are merely bestowing upon their students time, guidance and community in developing their talents, British faculty almost seem to see themselves as literary intercessors, with an active role to play in exposing as much of their students' best work to the publishing community as possible. The specific methods they have institutionalized to ensure that this happens will be described in detail in chapter three, but it is important to note that not only have these methods been institutionalized but a general attitude toward sharing publishing opportunities has been institutionalized in these programs as well. For example, after novelist and biographer Richard Francis brought his editor in to speak to his graduate students at Bath Spa University, we all retired to a nearby pub, where he and I chatted amiably for a few moments and then he excused himself because, "there are still a few students who haven't talked to her yet and I *must* introduce them."

In the undergraduate programs I investigated, a corollary attitude was echoed by leading faculty, and this was the understanding that not all the students pursuing a writing degree would become published writers but they all wanted to work in the world of words, a world to which these faculty felt it their responsibility to help them gain entry. Key to this philosophy is the recognition, shared by most of us who teach in the field, that the development of literary ability can be a slow, uneven process that may in fact take many years. As this process unfolds (and even if it means students eventually decide their passions lie elsewhere) it is critical to provide them with the knowledge and skills to pursue meaningful careers in the creative industries.

In fact, these differences in career goals are also the same differences that render the hand-me-down pedagogies of the graduate creative writing program such a poor fit for

13

undergraduate writing programs. Graduate students in creative writing today are by most accounts much further along in their development as writers, indeed, as human beings, and have self-selected graduate study as a means to further accelerate that growth. As such, they are more suited to the intense workshop pedagogies that privilege the act and product of writing above all else. Undergraduates, however, may benefit from a less specialized, more taught curriculum that includes not only genre-specific workshop courses but also broader introductions to the realm of creative writing studies and to professional and new media writing.

Finally, taking a cue from a small country for whom literature and writing remain culturally prized, this book enumerates not only options for reform in undergraduate and creative writing programs but also calls for more direct involvement of these programs in building a more literate society. Dana Gioia (2007) and others repeatedly strike death knells for the place of reading in our society. Yet, if we continue to support a culture that continually reinscribes the notion of the artist as an individual genius who springs miraculously and fully formed virtually from birth (and only coincidentally from a middle or upper class background) at the expense of deliberately cultivating writers from among a burgeoning youth culture that ranges across race and class and whose definition of literacy has expanded to include genre novels, graphic novels, spoken word poetry and web content, the very idea of a literate culture will die on the vine, a host of talented writers outside the "mainstream" forever undiscovered.

There are preventative measures that can be implemented by creative writers and writing programs which can avert this calamity, some of which have already been taken (author Dave Eggers' *826 Valencia* community writing centers come immediately to mind) and need even more support, and some which have yet to be created. These measures will require the concentrated resources of a creative society united in its determination to expand the scope of culture and literature as well as the similarly concentrated efforts of those of us who write and who teach writing to ensure that this form of artistic expression is available to anyone who seeks it, regardless of race or socioeconomic status. The last chapter of this book will look at these programs, such as Eggers' brainchild and the well-established Arvon Foundation in the UK, in light of how they can be adapted, expanded and their support institutionalized in growing the next generation of readers and writers.

Toward a culture of reflection
With ever-increasing numbers of students pursuing creative writing in higher education and the potential as well as the responsibility such numbers engender, our field itself is at another crossroads. The stakes, then, are high as they always are with a generation of students at the center. Just as community remains important for writers but is no longer enough, the controlling myth of the writer in the garret, toiling in isolation and insulated from the cultural shifts of the outside world no longer serves our students. This book has been written for the corresponding generation of writers and teachers who are more eager than ever to accept the challenge and raze the garret with what park rangers might describe as a controlled burn, using the innovative programs described in these pages as starting points in

constructing, in its place, a more resilient, environmentally responsive space for the development and sustenance of young writers and literary culture.

The fact is, changes that will benefit creative writing programs and their students are many in number and as unique as the individuals and the institutions executing them. What is perhaps most important, however, is that the field of creative writing in higher education move towards a culture of reflection, one that embraces continuous improvement, rather than the fall-back defensiveness that positions another wagon in the wide circle against criticism and continues to institutionalize unconsidered tradition over considered innovation.

Mark McGurl locates the fork at which writing programs took a more conservative turn in the nascent Iowa Writers' Workshop during and immediately after the Second World War, when two American literary "regionalisms, Midwestern and Southern," moving in opposite directions, crossed paths (2009, p. 151). Iowa founder and father of the modern writing program, Paul Engle, embodied the Midwestern regionalist who felt institutions must look "outward and s[eek] prestige through expansion," while Southern traditionalists, exemplified by writers like Flannery O'Connor, felt that institutions should embody "tradition, a place where the authority of past practices is contained and conserved" (p. 151). Ultimately, bolstered by O'Connor and New Critics Robert Penn Warren and Cleanth Brooks, the Southern traditionalists won the day.

Unconsidered tradition is simply no longer a luxury for creative writing programs, if it ever was. To be successful in the twenty-first century, in the midst of the "most significant change in human expression in human history" (Miller 2008), our students must stay abreast of a stunningly variable culture that privileges the ability to use information critically and remain open to new ways of doing old things, to constantly revise themselves and their abilities. As stewards of programs that cannot even begin to predict the writing worlds these students will face twenty, ten or even five years from now, it is our responsibility to build nimble creative writing programs that do the same, asking no less of ourselves than the world asks of them. Certainly, the Paul Engle characterized in McGurl's history would approve.

Notes from the Field
Storming the Garret

Sometimes the question comes from one of our writing majors. A senior who thinks he knows a few things about putting pen to paper. We'll call him Payton. He's stacked up accolades for his writing since he was in elementary school and regularly publishes prize-winning poems in the campus literary magazine. Maybe his mother is an English teacher, heck, maybe both his parents are English teachers.

'What if, you know, someone's just not very talented? Should you keep humouring them? Shouldn't you just,' at this point he lowers his voice to a conspiratory whisper, 'tell them to hang it up?'

Clearly from the cynical half-grin with which Payton delivers this question, he already has several classmates in mind. And of course, the freedom he feels to ask it at all reveals that he does not believe this category includes him.

Sometimes it comes from a student like Jessica. Jessica is a cheerfully-dressed, dewy-eyed education major who has wanted to be a teacher from the time she lined up her stuffed animals and patiently taught them their letters with a toy blackboard.

'What if,' Jessica asks tentatively, 'you have a student who just isn't a very good writer? How do you tell them?'

Jessica plans to teach third grade.

No matter how many times I hear this question in my creative writing pedagogy course, phrased in any number of ways, blatant, subtle, unapologetic, I am never prepared. My heart tightens, contracts like a clenched fist, while I

will my countenance to remain unmoved. I do not like to
think of myself as a teacher who tells her students, if only
by expression, what to think or what to parrot back to me,
preferring, instead, in the slow unraveling of the semester,
to win them over to my side by setting information out
and encouraging them to form their own conclusions.
Answers rise to my throat immediately but I bite them
back, swallow them down. If I am to be convincing, I
know I must temper my reactions, moderate my emotions.
And because I am a writer, I know I need time to reflect
on my beliefs, write them into being, measure my words.

Read on as I begin to try.

Sometimes, at the start of teaching this very same class,
I ask students to close their eyes and imagine a writer,
writing. Then I list a composite of what they describe
when they open their eyes. The usual suspects tumble out
of their mouths.

'A single, lonely figure.'

'A garret.'

'A dripping candle stub and a feathered pen.'

'Who's writing?' I ask. 'Is it a man or a woman?'

'A man,' they admit, although most of them are women.

Close your eyes, I ask them again. Where do you write?

In cafés, they tell me. In their dorm rooms, in the gym,
in the laundromat, at the bus stop.

Jane Austen, I tell them, was forced to write in the family
dining room. Edith Wharton and Truman Capote wrote
in bed. Raymond Carver wrote in his car.

I have written in a station wagon outside Kentucky Fried
Chicken, in coffee houses and on trains. In classrooms,
always in classrooms.

I composed part of this chapter 36,000 feet over the

Atlantic between my nine-year-old and my five-year-old, who were gorging on the Cartoon network via British Airways television. I have never written in a garret. I don't know anyone who has. Yet, if I am honest I must admit that when I close my own eyes and imagine a writer, I too see a man, a garret, a dripping candle stub and a feathered pen.

A centuries old myth, bred perhaps into our very DNA, it reminds us of everything we are not. Perhaps this is why so many of us anoint ourselves gatekeepers, holding the masses back from storming the garret doors. We must keep it pristine, this myth. Unsullied.

Catalogues don't label them poet blouses for nothing. They do it so they can charge us more for them. They are precious, poet blouses.

I have a friend, Bill, who's in his eighties, a learned, distinguished person. A gentleman of many talents, he was once a prosperous, award-winning florist. A discriminating reader, too, I glean from the titles on his bookshelf, mostly on British and American history.

When I can, I try to get him to tell me stories about growing up in our little Southern town in the twenties and thirties – when it truly was little. A relative newcomer compared to Bill, I have only lived here for ten years and I am curious. One of his best friends as a boy became the local jeweller. He went to high school around the corner from his home, when the district was small enough to contain all twelve grades on one patch of land. He ran with a gang of kids that were all only children, singletons we'd call them today, and, in the absence of any siblings, they remained close for the rest of their lives.

'These are great stories,' I tell him. 'You really ought to write them down.'

He frowns, waves a weathered hand to swat away an imaginary fly. 'I'm no writer,' he says.

'But they're wonderful stories,' I persist. 'I enjoy them.'

What hangs, silent, in the air between us is that one day they'll be lost forever if he doesn't write them down.

Still, the answer for him is all too clear. He is not a writer. Only a writer can tell these stories. His stories.

Here is my story. I have loved to write since I was a little girl, making up rhymes and stories, employing a stapler, scissors and yellow legal paper to fashion an editor's visor (remember those?) when I was five. Over the years, I tried desperately to write something that would attract my teachers' accolades but for the most part, they remained unimpressed.

When I was in fourth grade, I won first place and a camera in a school-wide writing contest. 'I was so surprised to see Stephanie had won that award,' my teacher, Mrs Benson said when she ran into my mother not long after at the Price Chopper. I was standing right beside them, holding tight to the silver shopping cart, and yet it was as if I was not even there.

We wrote a lot in Mrs Benson's class that year, responding to Renoir paintings (Studies of the Berard Children was my favourite) or Barry Manilow songs. Each time I turned in an essay or story I hoped she would write something encouraging on it. Each time the piece was returned without comment.

Of course she was surprised.

There were many more Mrs Bensons over the span of my school career. Nonetheless, today I am a writer and a writing teacher.

'Ah-ha!' you say. 'You persisted because you are a born

writer and we all know writers are born, not made.'

Not so fast. I'll tell you why I'm here. I'm here because for every Mrs Benson there was a Sean O'Connell, the handsome, dashing friend of my uncle, who marvelled at the journal I carried around, asking each time he saw me, 'So, how's the writer?' There was a Mrs Stone, who was not my English teacher but who often took me aside in seventh grade homeroom and, nodding toward the blue books I scribbled in furiously then, would ask, thirty-nine-year-old to thirteen-year-old, writer-to-writer, 'What'cha working on?'

There were my parents, who might have shuddered a little when I asked to subscribe to Writer's Digest at fifteen but who never let on. There was my uncle himself (at nine years my senior, more like a revered older brother) who began giving me inspirational writing books for Christmas when I was still in high school.

All of them, and those I do not have space to mention, are the reasons for my career today. And it's a good thing, too, because those Mrs Bensons pack a mean punch.

A powerful punch. Simply because she was my teacher. It's just as Spiderman says, with great power comes great responsibility, something any future teacher must consider.

Let's try another hypothetical situation. Let's say that in addition to being a teacher, you are also a coach, a duality not uncommon for many teachers today. You coach sixth grade soccer. Let's say they're an earnest group but none of them have been playing long and as far as you can tell, there's not a Mia Hamm among them.

What are your responsibilities here? How do you use your power?

Do you tell the kids to surrender their black and white balls and return their uniforms? Or do you show them some moves, show them you believe in them, and see what happens?

I know what I'd choose. Perhaps they'll surprise me. I like surprises.

Maybe you don't like sports metaphors. Vickie Spandel, in *The Nine Rights of Every Writer*, puts it this way: "When a child takes his first tentative steps and falls, we applaud the walking and cheer for him when he gets up. We never say, 'Well, he's no walker, that's for sure.' We know – we believe – that he will not only walk but run, climb mountains, ski the steepest slopes, dance the tango" (p. 63).

That's right. We believe.

At this point some of you might be thinking: 'What a flake. I'll just humour her just like she humours those poor, talentless students. Obviously she can't handle the truth.'

Yet another story, second hand. When I was pursuing my MFA I was fortunate to take several courses with writer and NPR book reviewer Allan Cheuse, a kind, bearish man who looks a little like Judd Hirsch. Once, in a bar after class, a few of us pressed him about the other students he'd taught. What were they doing? Had they made it as writers?

He allowed that some had. He threw out some names. Sure, we nodded eagerly, we recognized them.

'But this is the thing,' he told us. 'They weren't always the ones I'd thought were the most talented early on. You learn, if you teach long enough, that it's not always easy to predict who will succeed and who will choose to follow another path.' He paused and took a long sip from his red wine. 'I'm just glad I kept my mouth shut.'

So, you learn to appreciate surprises and you learn to keep your mouth shut. And, if you do this long enough, you also learn to be frank about what 'good' writing is and where it comes from. You learn this because sometimes the most unlikely student, the one whose work has so far utterly failed to captivate, will suddenly write the most beautiful sentence. And then, just to prove that this is no freak accident, she'll write another one. She's stretching, she's making moves and if you're truthful with yourself, completely truthful, you admit that if she works hard, if she builds on those two beautiful sentences, if she's in it for the long haul, she might make it further than you have ever dreamed.

It's a humbling realization. There's no way of knowing what will happen ultimately, but witnessing this over and over again, as I have in the last fifteen years, you begin to think that maybe it's not the word 'writer' that's so precious. Maybe it's the act of writing. And maybe that act should belong to everyone.

Some years after my MFA, when I was on a committee to interview candidates for a creative writing position, we had the opportunity to interview a well-known writer and teacher, one who had spent nearly 30 years building a major graduate program for a flagship state university (no, not Iowa). He had gone as far as he could where he was and he was looking to finish his career somewhere else.

'Is there ever a situation,' one of us asked, 'where you might tell a student to give up? That they have no future as a writer?'

'Absolutely not,' he told us. 'I tell them it's hard. It is hard, no matter what kind of talent you have at that particular moment. But no, I'd never tell anyone to give up. I've been wrong too many times.'

He was hired.

There's just one more story I have saved for last. The story of James Marshall, well-known illustrator and author of countless children's books, some of which may have been fixtures of your youth. Remember *George and Martha* and *Miss Nelson is Missing*? Ah yes, the faint smile of recognition. A beloved friend of the legendary Maurice Sendak, who considered him an artistic peer, many of Marshall's books remain in print decades after their initial publication, to the delight of generations of children everywhere. Someday, perhaps even your own.

As a child, James Marshall loved to draw. He filled page after page, just for the pure joy of it. Then in second grade, his teacher gazed at one of his sketches and, shaking her head, pronounced, 'Jimmy, you're no artist.'

So James Marshall put down his pen and his sketchbook. He would not pick them up again until he was twenty-eight years old, when he began drawing to relieve tension. Fortunately, his work found its way to readers not long after.

In 1993 James Marshall died from AIDS. He was forty-one.

It's a simple equation. You do the math.

Eight. Twenty-eight. Forty-one.

I hope that answers your question.

Chapter Two

Undergraduate Creative Writing Programs

In early 2003, the *Chronicle of Higher Education* published an essay by a woman in a position similar to my own. Fern Kupfer was a creative writing professor whose students, she despaired, longed to live the kind of life she led, making their living in the world of words, reading and writing, writing and reading. What the poor things didn't realize, she wrote quite frankly, for an audience of her peers in a publication her students would probably never read, was that they couldn't. The kind of work she did, this professor implied, was reserved for the elect, whether by faith or works, and her students, she was fairly sure, could never be among these. Given the difficult odds facing anyone who wants to be a writer, Kupfer is extremely skeptical of writing programs in higher education, yet rationalizes that her students still "get their money's worth" because what she really teaches is "writing appreciation," for students who will never be able to "do what she does," because, as she puts it, "I am already doing it" (p. B5).

I was appalled. I taught the same kinds of students, many of whom had fallen hard for the writing life for the first time (though most of them had been secretly writing for years), and they were in love. Crazy in love. I believed it was my job to set them on a path to do just the kind of work I was doing, or to make it possible for them to make a creative living in some way with words, with writing and reading, if that was what they wanted to do. Seven years later, I have former students who make their living as: film and music critics for the state-wide newspaper; web content developers for creative services and advertising firms; teachers at secondary schools and universities; staff members for national literary magazines; editors and writers for a long list of regional publications; and so many technical writers that I have literally lost count. In the narrowest sense of the term, only a few of these students are "literary artists," but many of them are writers, who continue to write and publish their work, and all of them have done what they have set to do and what I have done: forged satisfying livelihoods working with words. At this moment, our writing program is less than ten years old, our undergraduate creative writing major less than two, but based on this list of students who are sustaining themselves in creative lives, I fully expect to be able to count those with published books among them soon. Of course, unless these students achieve the success of J.K. Rowling or Stephen King, they probably won't quit their day jobs. After all, neither Fern Kupfer nor I have.

Certainly, my students start out with serious misconceptions about the artist's life, mainly that it is characterized by alternating swaths of quiet contemplation and leisurely wordsmithery that fit neatly into an eight-hour day while simultaneously putting a late-model hybrid car in every garage and a gourmet meal in every granite-trimmed kitchen. Late youth and early adulthood is rife with misconceptions fueled by inexperience. But youth and their misconceptions about reality aside, if I thought I was educating my students to pursue a life like mine, only to lead them to a locked door, I couldn't do it. I'd have to find another line of work.

At the time, however, Professor Kupfer's essay made me think seriously about the creative life that I was privileged to lead and how I had gotten there, as well as the kind of trail I was leaving for the students who hoped to follow me. I had already begun to think and write about the paucity of direction I'd received in my own artist's education – a recommendation here, an offer to "put in a good word" there – enough to realize just how much I'd persisted, fumbling in darkness – or at least dusk – to find my way as a writer and teacher. I had already begun to realize that if my students were to have it "better" than I did, a change in pedagogy, in the writing program curriculum, indeed, in educational philosophy was necessary. What I didn't understand was how large scale those changes would be, larger than I could have imagined at the time, with Web 2.0 only winking over the horizon. All I knew was that for the time being, what mattered was my undergraduate students and teaching them not only to write but also how to make creative lives. Utterly unaware at that point that I stood on the tip of a submerged iceberg, all I knew was that forging a better path for my students than the one I had had, started with me.

Now seems a good time to step back and define some terms. When I say the artist's life, I mean the artist's life writ large, a life that in one capacity or another means creating something that did not exist before, and, in the case of writing, to execute this act via words. There are numerous ways to do this, to realize one's creative instincts; teaching writing is just one of them. As early as 1997, Carol Lloyd argued in *Creating a Life Worth Living* that Western culture tends to hold a narrow, either/or conception of the artist's life. *Either* we spend our days painting masterpieces or inserting and removing commas from our next Pulitzer Prize winner *or* we abandon our creative needs for the "practical" livelihood our parents warned us we'd need to fall back on. Largely because of these parental admonitions and black-and-white cultural expectations, we rarely explore the area in between.

My journey to build a better curriculum for my undergraduates was then, and continues to be, a work in progress. But with each semester I become more aware of the need to provide my students with the skills and the confidence to make their way into their creative livelihoods in that "in-between" space, and more determined to seek out the coursework and the teaching strategies that will scaffold them. This need is perhaps even more urgent at the state institution where I teach, populated with many first-generation college students for whom the next step down on the economic ladder is menacingly close, and whose parents' constant worries about their vocations form the backbeat of their lives. These students do not need a steady, exclusive diet of teacher-centered workshops led by a writer who is herself given to musing whether her subject can even be taught (if you're thinking this subject was put to bed long ago and I'm beating a dead horse, look no further than Dan Barden's article in the March/April 2008 issue of *Poets and Writers* magazine). No, these students need a plan. A plan of study and a curriculum that will allow them to learn the craft of writing *and* give them the skills which will sustain them as writers after they graduate. Some may call such a plan itself too narrow, too vocational, asserting that as long as one teaches craft and "writing appreciation" the rest takes care of itself. I disagree.

But really (wink, wink) can it really be taught?
Unfortunately, this question has persisted into the twenty-first century even as writers like myself and Kelly Ritter (2007) or scholar Greg Light (2002), who conducted robust research on the question, have struggled mightily to put it, like a recalcitrant toddler, to bed. The answer is yes. In fact, it was Light's research that proved what most of us who teach the subject already knew. In his longitudinal study of creative writing students at institutions of higher education in the United Kingdom, students did in fact exhibit learning in their creative writing curriculum by passing through a series of developmental stages in their conception of creative writing. Light terms these: i) Releasing; ii) Documenting (limited); iii) Documenting (extended); iv) Narrating (limited); v) Narrating (extended); vi) Critiquing.

As any teacher of creative writing will recognize, beginning writing students in the "Releasing" stage often view writing as a "personal, private creation" that works simply by being "released". Any concern for the reader is "detached" from the writing, the writer fails to understand the idea of the reader. Light goes on to describe, in the first of the two "Documenting" stages (limited), how the advanced beginner may accept the idea of a reader at the receiving end of their writing, but view how the reader receives their work as a "situation over which they feel they have little control." In the next documenting stage (extended) the writer begins to have an "extended sense of reader" and an awareness of making the writing meaningful for them.

In the next stage, Narrating (limited), the student writer begins to demonstrate an integrated conception of the reader with regard to both their "perception and practice of writing," which leads student writers to consider *structuring* their inner narration *for* the reader, even if their understanding of how to execute this structure is limited. However, in Narrating (extended) the writer moves toward a consolidated integration of the reader through "a more extensive and cohesive use of form [and] convention," even beginning to consider the idea of "deploying" writing techniques to enhance the reader's experience. Finally, in the Critiquing stage, Light suggests that all of these conceptions converge; writers understand how to express "original material" and to "integrate the reader" within the act of writing, both within a critical perspective and a metacognitive understanding of how expression and reader response can work together

Thus, we can say that Light's research supports what we already see in our classrooms. If teaching and learning mean passing through a series of developmental stages in knowledge and conception, then creative writing can and is being taught and learned in higher education. What's more, understanding how creative writing is learned can help us determine how to teach it *better*: specifically, how to teach students at different levels in their learning and how to prod them to the next.

Moreover, once we admit that creative writing can be taught, it becomes incumbent on us to teach it and to teach it well, like any other subject. No longer can we hide behind the academic face-saving "but it's an unteachable subject" mantra. Rather, we must continually re-examine our pedagogy and our curriculum to ensure that we are teaching our students both about the life and craft of writing and the multifaceted, ever-changing world of creative industry in which they will ply their trade.

Teaching the "real" writing life

It is a fact universally acknowledged (but hopefully not encouraged) by most teachers of creative writing that the heads of undergraduate or beginning writers virtually teem with the myths they've spent their whole lives absorbing about writers and writing via popular culture including: that writing is easy; that perfect first drafts spring from pens or keyboards fully formed; that writing itself is reserved for crazed, isolated, drug-addicted "geniuses." The early stages of any undergraduate writing curriculum involve a fair amount of debriefing, then, in order to move students beyond the garret and the cult of individual genius while at the same time introducing them to real-world artistic practice. At this point, for example, it is more important than ever to draw back the curtain on the wizard and show undergraduates the many invention tricks writers rely upon to get started and to keep the well of inspiration at an optimum level. Loosely translated, moreover, this means undergraduate writers, especially first or second year students, need to spend *at least* as much time both in and out of class actually writing (with the teacher modeling and writing along with them) as they do discussing the work of their peers and having their own critiqued, focusing on process as much as or more than product because a writer's process is still so varied and largely, mythically, misunderstood.

Undergraduates or novice writers also need to learn as much as possible about that vast territory known as the "writing life" by being encouraged to read writers' biographies and autobiographies and committing themselves to the study of the artistic development of writers that can inform their own work. They need to be exposed to as many writers at as many different stages in their careers as possible – not just to hear them read from their work but also to learn *how* they crafted their writing lives and what those lives entail. As Wendy Bishop points out in *Released Into Language*, it is important for students to learn how varied writers' lives are, that there is no one way to write or pursue a writing career (1998). Many schools hold reading series to expose students to the *creative* work of different writers, but it is just as important to expose students to these writers' daily lives and career trajectories. We know that it's difficult to make a living solely by writing but we also know that it's possible to keep body and soul together in any number of satisfying creative ways *in addition* to writing; that there are, in fact, as many ways to do this as there are people doing it.

Perhaps you have already noticed that the ideal undergraduate writing curriculum is, to coin the British phrase, more *taught* than the graduate curriculum, which makes sense when one considers that its constituency is largely uninitiated to the literary life. It goes without saying, then, that the amorphous "workshop method" works best as only one part of a spectrum of teaching techniques and classroom exercises used in the creative writing classroom, rather than the centerpiece. Writing workshops, as they were conceived and developed at the University of Iowa and then spread, were designed almost exclusively for graduate students, those who were much further along in their journey as writers. In fact, as they largely developed after the Second World War, they also catered, especially in the US, to returning soldiers who, funded by the GI Bill (money provided by the government to bankroll their education), seized the opportunity to finance their love of writing and literature and make sense of their war experiences in writing. The workshop clothes fashioned for these more mature, worldly writers simply don't fit undergraduates, who require an entirely different curricular line.

Undergraduates, for example, tend to have, according to Priscila Uppal, "limited experience and a restricted range of responses to authorship" (2007, p. 48). As a result, "the task of the creative writing teacher is to give them exercises that *expand and open* their creativity." While they may resist these at first, a series of shorter exercises, Uppal argues, is more likely to show students the range available to them than the few longer pieces turned in and "workshopped" in a traditional workshop. Wendy Bishop, moreover, encourages "risk taking and revision by deferring product grades to final portfolios" (2005, p. 111). In my own courses, I encourage risk taking by focusing all of the grades (yes, all of them) on the quality of the critical introductions students write to all of their work and on the quality of their written responses to the work of other students. I do not grade their creative work, although I always respond to it in detail. This practice has the result of freeing "grade-anxious" students to take risks and try genres they have never explored before. For example, students frequently tell me, "I've never written much poetry before but I decided to try it with this assignment." This is just what I want to hear – first- and second-year students should be trying a smorgasbord of genres, not limiting themselves to those that get them positive feedback and preserve their grade point average.

With the increase in creative writing majors across the higher education landscape, good news in general for the future of literary culture, it is hardly insensitive to observe that not all undergraduates will become "writers" in the narrowest sense of the word. Maggie Butt, Head of Media at Middlesex University, says it best when she allows that "most of our students won't become prize-winning novelists and poets, any more than all fine arts graduates are hung in the Tate or music graduates play with the London Philharmonic" (2008, p. 37). Virtually all students who seek out these programs, however, *do* want to do work that stimulates and engages their creative selves. In the early part of a new century, characterized by media that morph at breathtaking speed (blogging>myspace>youtube>?), meeting this desire requires a supple curriculum that teaches students not only invention and craft but also a creatively entrepreneurial mindset that can adapt to these changes. It is an old but inherently true saw that we may not even be able to envision the world in which we are preparing our students to live and work, yet we must give them the tools and the habits of mind to thrive in it.

The kind of curriculum that prepares students to be responsive to evolving creative economic milieus is at once craft driven (good writing = good writing = good writing) and real-world based (i.e. writing for the web requires an entirely different skill set from writing for a print audience). At the mid to upper levels, moreover, such a curriculum must aim to give students every opportunity to explore hands-on real-world creative writing situations, including, but not limited to: editing and publishing online and print magazines; freelance writing; and connecting with the local, regional and national arts communities. For example, undergraduate writing majors at the University of Central Arkansas, where I teach, must all take a course called Writing for New Technologies I, that gives them a basic sense of the principles for online writing, principles that take into account visual design theory and the ways in which the web has changed the way people read. If they are interested, they may elect to pursue the topic further in Writing for New Technologies II and III, that latter course involving real-world experience designing documents for local companies and non-profits.

A survey of ninety-six college creative writing programs in the UK revealed that about half taught these kinds of professionally oriented courses (Butt et al. 2008). According to Scott Brook, in Australia, the creative industries "curriculum seeks to establish the value of creativity in terms of both the inculcation of general or transferable skills required by a contemporary 'creative workforce' and as the training and qualification of personnel for specific cultural industries" (2009, pp. 8–9). In 2007, moreover, the Australian Publishers' Association developed a "curriculum review and accreditation process that enables qualifying...writing programs with an industry-focus to carry its imprimatur" (p.15). While it may be tempting to scoff at this vocational focus, Brook's report also points out that programs with this focus provide especially valuable and attractive degrees for students with artistic leanings who also hail from a lower socio-economic status and for whom the safety net of a creative industry focus is a palpable benefit. Also for this reason perhaps, Geoff Becker from the University of Towson (Maryland) describes his institution's emphasis on such courses as particularly attractive for the regional, first generation college students that populate his institution "who don't really know what they want to do, they just know they like writing" (2010).

Consequently, a once exotic course in the traditional creative writing curriculum, the course in editing and publishing, often linked to a campus literary magazine, is now a necessary component of the undergraduate creative writing program. What's more, in our increasingly visual culture, the aesthetic and technical elements of document production and presentation need to be reinforced in every creative writing course. Even introductory creative writing courses must encourage students to present their work via creative and visually appealing individual chapbooks and class publications. Through advanced versions of these assignments and incorporations of basic document design and technology, upper division creative writing courses should reinforce the idea that students *thoughtfully* consider the visual and digital presentation of their work. At the very least, these students will graduate with marketable publishing skills and at the most, they'll be empowered to take charge of getting their own work into the world.

Exploring publication

In a shifting environment where students are expected to be media savvy at younger and younger ages, it is no longer realistic to tell novice students not to worry about the nuts and bolts of publishing their work. This does not mean that undergraduates should send their juvenilia out en masse or that we should encourage them to consider publication as the ultimate end when they sit down to write. But we do them a disservice by mystifying the world of publication and trying to keep them innocent of it for as long as possible.

Not long ago, I was one of those teachers who, when beginning writers asked about publication, would likely reply, "you don't need to worry about that yet." But over time, I've come to believe that it's irresponsible to send students out into the writing world with so little knowledge of the marketplace that they have no clue how to enter it once they *are* ready to begin the long journey of submission, rejection and occasionally, publication. Such ignorance also renders them vulnerable to the increasingly sophisticated tactics of vanity and subsidy publishing, predatory agents, publishers, book doctors and the like. While it is hard to argue that the early efforts of any writer should be thrown to the literary lions, there is no reason not to teach students about their appetites and the laws of the pride. Bath Spa Creative Writing tutor Mimi Thebo has created a thriving pair of courses in marketing and publishing, spotlighted later in this chapter, that provides a model for achieving this end.

Creative enterprise and the arts community

Students in an undergraduate creative writing curriculum already know that they're different from their counterparts in, say, Accounting or Physical Therapy simply by a tally of tattoos and piercings. However, growing up in a culture that is unlikely to privilege artists as anything more than the rarest of hothouse orchids, most of them have no idea how to translate these differences into fulfilling careers. As the son of a visual artist, for example, American writer Jonathan Lethem already had a model for cultivating his creative gifts. Few of our students have that advantage. It is up to us to provide it for them, right alongside lessons in style and craft. Here, books like Daniel Pink's *A Whole New Mind*, Richard Florida's *The Rise of the Creative Class*, Eric Maisel's *Fearless Creating* and *The Creative*

Life and last, but perhaps most important, Carol Lloyd's *Creating a Life Worth Living*, come into play, deserving just as prominent a place on our course reading lists as craft texts by writing gurus Anne Lamott, John Gardner, Stephen King, or Natalie Goldberg. *Creating a Life Worth Living* lends itself especially well to the rhythm of an entire semester, as it helps students to explore their strengths as artists and then to develop multiple plans for expressing them via rewarding occupations.

In terms of creative enterprise, moreover, undergraduate programs could be doing more to help students apply their creative skills to interface with the outside world and apply their ingenuity to the "business of writing," or the arts at large. Steve May and Mimi Thebo, at Bath Spa University, created just such a program when they determined that their capstone course had become "very safe and contained. Students seemed to see it as just an opportunity to write a bit more of what they'd written before (i.e. 'I'd thought I'd write three short stories')" (Butt 2008, p.38). Thebo and May wanted to push graduating students "as far as we could, to get them accustomed to the 'business' content of writing and deal with it" (p. 38). They sought to encourage students to be "adventurous, to follow their own interest," for academic credit, as long as their project could relate "in some realistic way to the world outside."

Launched in 2005, their course, known as the Creative Enterprise Project, quickly gained buy-in with subjects outside creative writing (for example, Cultural Studies and History) which enlarged the range of activities the students could engage in. "Assessment of the project," May wrote, is "designed to be flexible" to avoid forcing students "into the thirteen-week teaching box mindset ... " Students may well start their project before the beginning of the semester and end it well after. Consequently, the grade for the course comes via "1. an approved project plan, 2. a presentation to peers and 3. "a project report, length and nature to be negotiated with the tutor, which captures what the student has already done and what they plan to do in the future." Finished projects have included a study of "freelancing in sitcom writing and journalism," the renovation of a letter press, the production of a promotional DVD for a national charity and the organization of a poetry festival.

In *A History of Professional Writing Instruction in American Colleges: Years of Acceptance, Growth and Doubt*, Katharine Adams reports that "most of the graduates who are employed today for their writing skills...have studied... advanced courses in journalism, technical writing...business writing, and creative writing" (p. 36). Most of us believe these words; we wouldn't teach writing if we didn't want it to be an important part of the lives our students are embarking on. Rather than cringe when one of them tells us she wants to "do just what you do," it is incumbent upon us, as teachers and as stewards of undergraduate creative writing programs, to enlarge our students' ideas of what it means to live creative lives, whether as a college writing professor, a web journalist or a music reviewer, and to construct a table big enough to give everyone a place. Read on for ideas from two vanguard undergraduate programs that have developed practices that do just that: enlarge the idea of the writing life for the baccalaureate writing student.

Program Spotlight: Arkatext
We initially developed Arkatext, an annual weeklong series of readings and craft talks, to demonstrate that New

York and LA were not the only sites of literary talent, that in fact, the vibrant literary scene in Arkansas meant a growing number of writers were making their living by the pen in our students' own backyards. To date, the series, which features three Arkansas writers in different genres, has brought in a new trio of accomplished writers each year, many of them nationally recognized. It's been eight years and we haven't reached the bottom of the well yet.

During craft lectures, many of the writers share their creative lives with our students. For example, in describing how he was finally able to write successfully full time after a number of years as a wildlife magazine editor, well-known sportsman and writer "Catfish" Sutton went to great pains to make sure his audience knew exactly what a typical month in his working life was like:

1. Wrote 15 blogs for ESPNOutdoors.com.
2. Wrote five 1000- to 1500-word newspaper articles.
3. Wrote fourteen 800- to 2500-word feature articles and columns for magazines.
4. Prepared a Powerpoint presentation for a crappie fishing seminar.
5. Wrote a press release for the fishing seminar and emailed it to 100 people who might help promote it.
4. Copy-edited 32 articles for Cabela's *Outfitter Journal*.
5. Spent 24-plus hours on the Internet compiling news sections for two magazines.
6. Edited three chapters of another author's book.
7. Completed the final chapters of a new book on catfishing, and prepared and submitted a photo package that will be used to illustrate that book.

8. Submitted four previously published articles for publication in magazines and on websites.

9. Spent four days gathering new product information at the Shooting, Hunting and Outdoor Trade (SHOT) Show in Las Vegas (and two days traveling there and back).

10. Spent two weeks reworking that information into a 36-page new product section for Stoeger Publishing's Shooter's Bible.

11. Spent 20 hours on the telephone requesting new product information I couldn't obtain at the SHOT Show

12. Reviewed more than 200 page proofs for Shooter's Bible.

13. Wrote 50 shooting tips for inclusion in Shooter's Bible.

14. Wrote and submitted queries for future articles to 12 outdoor magazines.

15. Wrote scripts for 12 television spots I'll host on ESPN television.

16. Spent two days searching for locales where those TV spots could be filmed.

17. Spent two days trying to catch various live baits that will be featured in the TV spots.

18. Spent two 12 hour days in front of the camera shooting 6 of the TV spots.

19. Completed and submitted invoices and contracts for the above items.

20. Wrote/answered an average of 65 emails daily.

21. Packaged and mailed more than 100 books sold through my website and mail order.

22. Spent one day preparing my Arkatext presentation.

23. Discussed assignments for 36 more magazine articles with editors.

24. Did several hours research for a new book on Arkansas fishing.

(Sutton 2008)

A program like Arkatext is relatively low budget (ours costs about $3,000) because it brings in local writers for one-day stints with no associated travel expenses. But the kind of insight and advice the students receive from writers like Sutton is priceless.

Program spotlight: Bath Spa University's "Toward Publication" and "Into Print"

In order to help her undergraduates become more publishing savvy, Mimi Thebo developed two intermediate courses at Bath Spa University: Toward Publication followed by Into Print. Not surprisingly, Thebo met with a great deal of resistance at first from fellow colleagues who fretted that "1. Editors would find queries from new writers annoying, 2. Our BA students would be hassling agencies and commissioning editors at fiction publishers and thus devalue the 'brand' of the Bath Spa MA, 3. Our students' writing would embarrass us if seen outside the university" (2008).

It took her two years, but Thebo managed to assure these naysayers that "magazine editors are used to getting queries and really don't mind saying no or ignoring inappropriate ones." What's more, few students would be approaching book editors because, according to Thebo, "very few of our BA students would have finished novels they were ready to market," and if they did, "we should be helping to assess these and if they [are] decent, help[ing] to market them." Finally Thebo convinced her colleagues that Bath Spa undergraduates were not "worse than other beginning writers ... they are very much better than the vast majority." Finally, Thebo explained that when she referred to publications, she did not mean big guns, such as Granta and the New Yorker, but smaller regional publications and competitions.

Resistance also arose among the students. Some, according to Thebo, "hate journalism, (although we make them learn it anyway ... they might like it better than stocking shelves three years on)." Some students find the publishing game ethically or aesthetically questionable – for these students, Thebo allows self-publishing, but they must still come up with a marketing plan. Other students find it jarring to be introduced to the less "romantic" side of the writing life. However, since their inception, these courses have proved their worth and have become part of a professional academic development course that will be compulsory for all writing students.

Notes from the Field
Grasping Ariadne's Thread[1]: Wendy Bishop's
Stories and My Own

> I am hoping for nothing less than to change our profession
> so that the parts of it which proved incredibly valuable for
> me and others like me are not lost to the kind of anger and
> difficulties you can hear in my story.
>
> (Wendy Bishop 1997, p. 245)

> Every reader's response to a writer's call can have its own
> startling, suggestive power.
>
> (Robert Coles 1990, p. xix)

Attempting to unravel the threads of Wendy Bishop's
influence in creative writing pedagogy is much like
unpacking creative writing theory and practice in the
ways she prodded us to do, questioning what had
previously seemed unquestionable. The strands are many
and varied: her unique perspective as a creative writer
and a compositionist, her championing of students and
teaching, and her writing about that teaching, "in praise
of pedagogy." But time and again, as I revisit her work,
what draw me back in are her story, her testimony, and
her courage in telling it, and the way these stories, like the
mythical golden thread Ariadne bestowed upon Theseus,
shed light on what had once been the shadowy labyrinth
of creative writing pedagogy.

Throughout her book, *Writing to Change the World*,
psychologist and writer Mary Pipher (2006) underscores
the power of story to elevate the human condition:

"Therapists tell stories [to] help our clients move forward. Change writers utilize stories in much the same way, to give people an emotional experience that opens their hearts and points them in new directions" (p. 96). Wendy Bishop was such a change writer, telling stories from a marginalized experience.

As part of a marginalized group, a woman in the male-dominated field of creative writing, Bishop wrote that we must "earn our authority *and* we must take it" (1997, p. 216). She found her authority in a voice that told stories to many who shared her membership in that group and for whom Bishop's experience was all too familiar

The first time I begin sustained work on this chapter, my eyes fill with tears – not just because I am sad at Wendy Bishop's absence, but also because I am grateful. Grateful for the space this book has given me to visit her again, to read and re-read her words. To re-read *Teaching Lives: Essays and Stories* for the first time since her death. In her introduction to *Teaching Lives*, composed, by my estimate, when she was about forty-three, Bishop writes that she is not "terribly old, though some days, I feel old enough." Reading this sentence myself at forty-one, the words take on new weight. In six years, Wendy Bishop would be gone.

I did not know Wendy Bishop in the way many of the authors in our field did; our professional relationship was rich but brief. Instead, I came to know Wendy Bishop at first through her words, words that spoke to me, words that would eventually compel me to invite her to our newly minted department of writing to share her work in composition and creative writing with our students and faculty. She came to the University of Central Arkansas for two days in the autumn of 1999, giving talks and readings, visiting creative writing classes. It was a visit that changed my life.

I was her escort and about as young and green as I could possibly be. Still, Bishop treated me with great professional respect, engaging me in discussions about writing and teaching, asking what I was working on. In fact, after the first day of her visit, she asked me how my publishing was going. I shared that I'd published a few articles, but that I'd recently gotten a rejection on a second rewrite of an essay and wasn't sure what to do next. She offered to take the essay to her hotel that night and read it, as well as the reviewers' comments, so that we could conference about it the next day. After I dropped her off at the Ramada, I had an epiphany: "My goodness," it suddenly occurred to me, "I think I'm being mentored."

One of the many stories Bishop tells is of a time in her youth when she was about to begin work at the Woolworths jewelry counter. She paints a vivid picture of her youthful self earnestly studying the handbook of procedures in order to be exceedingly well prepared for her new job. Bishop tells us this story to make the point that when she applied this earnestness to the academy, she found that there was no rule book and that whatever rules did exist were largely unspoken and sometimes contradictory. This story sets the stage for the others that will follow, stories that are familiar to anyone who knows Bishop's work and doubly familiar to those of us who have experienced similar narratives ourselves. For in telling the story of her time as a graduate student in writing, studying with famous writers, Wendy Bishop wrote that one of the rules she learned was that it was "understood that poets, like people in love, always behave badly, except on occasion" (Shapiro 1992, p. 55).

Yet she also intuited that "if I were to behave badly, then I would not be let into the club of women who swarmed the workshops, the famous writers' lunches, professors' trips. In the role of a bad girl – one wanting respect and attention for her writing – I would not be contributing to, I would be asking of. And that would not do" (Bishop 1997, p. 238).

These days, I'm a veteran visiting-writer-escort, and I'm happy to report that most of the guests are charming and generous. But nearly 10 years later, Bishop's gesture still stands out for its lack of precedence, underscored by the fact that I later discovered that I was not the only junior faculty member to whom she made this offer. My experiences with mentoring had, up to that point, been wildly uneven, due in part to the background I shared with Bishop, in both literature and creative writing. I had recently emerged from a PhD program that had been incredibly nurturing, where the faculty, most of whom were literature and composition professors, went out of their way to help me grow as a writer and a scholar, into a member of the professoriate. This experience was in bold contrast to that of my MFA program.

Let there be no mistake; it pains me to write this. The writers I studied with were good, kind, encouraging people, people who gave me $20 once to photocopy a story for class when I mentioned I was broke, people who put out a hand when I was new and young and scared. At the same time, whatever teaching and mentoring went on was far more social than anything else. It went on in the conversations I listened raptly to at the "famous writers' lunches, professors' trips" that I was, mostly, fortunate to be included in. It probably went on in the poker games that, as a woman and one who did not know the game, I was not. It sometimes went on during classes that were exclusively workshops or professor-led discussions of the work at hand. But it did not go on in the occasional independent study meeting with an individual faculty member, where it became clear that my work had not been read. It did not go on in the appointments that were scheduled and canceled, scheduled and canceled, sometimes after I'd commuted more than an hour by car and train each way to attend. It did not go on during my comprehensive oral exams, which were studied for, attended, and then canceled so many times that one of my professors finally admitted, "You're probably getting pretty tired of this." An understatement, of course, but at the time I just nodded meekly. Like Wendy Bishop, I did not want to be known as a "bad girl." Bad girls did not get invited to the lunches and dinners, and these were all I had.

Indeed, *Teaching Lives: Essays and Stories* is full of such tales. Stories of what it feels like to be the "other," where it is a given that "if you make it, you're a poet, if you fail, you're a woman poet" (Bishop 1997, p. 239), in first-year graduate workshops where students gathered at the feet of a famous, pipe-smoking, white-haired poet and in second-year workshops that consisted of hours of "meeting with a group of other aspiring poets not to be taught" (p. 239). Of being "momentarily mentored" (p. 239) in another workshop and advised not to use her first name, but, rather, to neutralize her gender with initials. Of studying with Karl Shapiro in particular, who wrote derisively of the unteachability of creative writing and mocked students who took classes with "No books, no tests, best grades guaranteed/A built-in therapy for all and sundry;/Taking in each other's laundry/No schedule, no syllabus, no curriculum/No more reading (knowledge has gone elsewhere)/Pry yourself open with a speculum/ And put a tangle in your hair" (1992, p. 27) yet who, she reports, during the year she "studied with him, returned no annotated texts, gave no tests, showed no grading standards, kept to no schedule, syllabus, designed no curriculum" (Bishop 1997, pp. 240–241).

A "speculum" – I don't know an adult woman who can hear or read that word without wincing. Deliberate on Shapiro's part? What poet would admit to a habit of word choice that was anything but? No, the intention of these words is very clear. It isn't just workshop students in general that Shapiro denigrates here, but the women, in particular, who often populate them.

Beyond this barb, however, Shapiro's poem also resonates for me decades later, when I read essays about the "unteachability" of creative writing: essays that indicate no awareness of the writers and scholars, such as Bishop and the authors in this volume, who have labored and continue to labor to reveal that creative writing can indeed be taught and to examine the ways in which the creative writing classroom might be revised to make the subject more teachable.

Bishop tells these stories because she suspects that she is not alone among those who are in "creative writing classes a lot but do not feel supported there. Some of us had internalized a destructive self-doubt" (p. 236). In fact, most of us, good girls (and boys) like Bishop, were silenced by such self-doubt, a silence that served only to isolate us in a system where poems and pervasive attitudes such as Shapiro's only further marginalized us as unworthy of instruction. Not surprisingly, then, we did not receive Bishop's words as "an attempt to pass into public [her] private dilemmas" (p. 120) but rather as a life preserver. At last, in Mary Pipher's (2006) words, our "deeply felt private experiences [were] given public legitimacy" (p. 189). The floodgates had been opened.

At this point, a more cynical reader might ask, if the situation in creative writing programs was so dire, what took so long for the emperor's nudity, so to speak, to become apparent? By the time her first essays on the subject were published creative writing had been institutionalized in US higher education, first officially via the University of Iowa, for more than 50 years. There are no easy answers.

I myself was a few years out of my MFA program before I encountered Bishop's work. During my MFA program, I'd found many of the unspoken rules unsettling, but as a "good girl" I was adept at submerging such feelings without a second thought. I saw what happened to "bad girls," who questioned the system, who demanded attention. Our teachers derided them when they left the room or at the bar after class. I knew I had a limited amount of time to learn what I could from this system. I had no intention of wasting my time trying to change it. Instead, I bowed my head, re-adjusted my blinders, and got to work.

In a conversation once, Jesse Lee Kercheval compared her graduate study in creative writing to "sharing an elevator with someone famous for a little while." At the time, I smiled in recognition and made a mental note of the witticism – it had never occurred to me that a program could or should be more than that. Until I discovered Wendy Bishop and started asking, "Why not?".

I read Bishop's stories, then, of her experiences in higher education, and with creative writing in particular, with a palpable sense of relief. For the first time, I understood that I was not alone, that my experiences had not been the result of my own inadequacies or even those of my teachers, but of a failed system that honored the product and its star creators in an economy of scarcity, rather than creating an empowering economy of process and, subsequently, wealth. For the first time, I broke my silence and began to speak out, to slide creative writing classrooms and their traditions under a microscope and study them for ways to make them better.

According to Bishop, it wasn't until she crossed over to composition and began to question the system that her stories emerged. She already had an instinct toward narrative; after all, she'd started out as a poet, but her turn toward composition studies gave her a burgeoning faith in the power of story. She wrote that her "somewhat unusual background as a graduate of both creative writing and comp programs" (p. 2) gave her a "flair for articulating the practical", but only by crossing "artificial," institutional borders was she "able to better compose [her] writing life" (p. 220). Although at first, and always, she wrote stories about her teaching to "encourage teachers to keep writing about teaching and their lives in teaching" (p. x) she quickly recognized that by "sharing published teaching stories [she] learned how to have a voice and a place in the composition community" (p. viii). She also saw that her more narrative style "allowed [her] to investigate ethical, political and writerly concerns more freely" (p. 216).

Bishop's expansive body of work attests that creative writing wasn't the only field that drew her intense scrutiny.

But it was a world in which she felt like an outsider, and it was this status, in particular, that compelled her to "testify" to her own "mis-education" because it was the "miseducational parts of that experience that drove me to improve the situation" (p. 236). In effect, her stories galvanize us by holding up a mirror to situations we had endured, validating our frustration; and then, most importantly, asserting that change was possible and we could be part of the solution. Even before Mary Pipher popularized the term *change writer*, Wendy Bishop realized that her stories could be catalytically "change-active" (p. 134).

Now, I teach creative writing to undergraduates, many of whom aspire to continue their study in graduate programs. I want their experiences, as both undergraduates and graduate students, to be different from mine. I want them to be mentored and shown the ropes, and I want their work and their evolution as writers attended to; in fact, I want my students to know that they deserve these considerations. Wendy Bishop's stories first gave me the inkling that this might be possible. Today, 10 years later, raised professionally on her stories and freed to tell my own, I *know* that it is. The creative writing scene in higher education is changing, perhaps not as quickly as I would like (nothing ever does), but still, it is changing. And my students have changed, in part, because Wendy's work inspired me to teach them better and to teach them to expect more from their experience in the creative writing classroom. I hope, too, that my own work and example have taught them the dangers of silence and freed them to speak. To tell their own story, as writers do.

Toni Morrison famously wrote, "The function of freedom is to free someone else,"(qtd. in Lamott 1995,

p. 193). Wendy Bishop saw that it was *through* her "training in rhetoric and composition, after my training in creative writing and *by* writing pedagogy" (p. 245; italics added) that she found herself as a writer. Yet it was in the story of her learning life, "one of sheer dogged insistence in the face of poor teaching," that she was actually composing herself, a daring act of composition that released others to tell their stories and compose *themselves*. In doing so, she also brought to light the hidden rule book, illuminating the invisible ink on its pages and inviting the rest of us to join her in examining it, describing what we find there, and, if necessary, agitating for change.

This book, as well as many other articles and collections, demonstrates the ways in which we continue to answer her invitation.

Note

1. Ariadne, daughter of King Minos of Crete and his wife Pasiphae, was in love with Theseus and promised to help him escape Daedalus' Labyrinth by giving him a ball of golden thread that she had received from the architect (Daedalus) himself. Unraveling the thread as he made his way through the labyrinth, once he had slain the Minotaur, Theseus needed only to follow the thread to find his way out (Connor 2005).

Chapter Three

Graduate Programs: Creative Writing Comes of Age

> I graduated from Iowa and Yale where there was a certain model. But that model is changing. We're seeing it as an opportunity.
> (Brighde Mullins, Director MA in Professional Writing, University of Southern California)

Although creative writing programs in higher education can trace their lineage back to the creation of the first MFA in Iowa in the 1940s, for the purposes of this book I'm going to date the real birth of the campus creative writing graduate program from the founding of the Associated Writing Programs in 1967, a collaboration of a dozen university writing programs to promote the presence of the writer on campus, especially in the face of resistance from literature departments, to overcome this resistance and "to provide publishing opportunities for young writers" (Fenza 2009).

The birth of a discipline is always exciting. Those present at the beginning undoubtedly feel the heady thrill of pioneers at the threshold of a vast uncharted wilderness, and rightly so. In the early years, as these pioneers machete their way through the overgrowth, not surprisingly, anything goes. In fact, as I mentioned in chapter one, at the dawn of creative writing's arrival in higher education, writers were so pleased to have found, in each other and in their students, fellow writers and sympathetic literature colleagues, a supportive community, that in its infancy, this community was more than enough. That is, it was enough for professors of creative writing to conduct the first several weeks of their courses by arriving with a stack of books from which they would read aloud select models of the genre at hand, reading that might continue until student work began to trickle in and the real labor of advice and critique could begin. It was enough, during these workshop sessions, simply to sit at a long table with these famous authors, hoping to catch pearls of wisdom from their mouths as they shared their take on the work under discussion, on writing and the creative life in general. *Most* of the time they had actually read the work under consideration, although occasionally, they hadn't (McNair 2008, Starkey 2010). Well, life happens and writers are good at winging it. It was enough really, to have a few years carved out from the non-literary world to focus on one's writing. Really, it was.

It's not any more. Today, with the surfeit of creative writing programs dotting the landscape, we can declare the frontier officially closed. The world is now saturated with creative writers and, although there are always a few curmudgeons who gripe about this state of affairs, I think it's a wonderful thing. In fact, I think it's the stuff of dreams, the stuff that a rich artistic culture is built upon.

However, I was also born in the same year that AWP formed and so I can safely attest: we are both middle-aged. Our carefree youth is over. We've got the kids to think about. Lots of them. Time to write, communities to support writing, advice from practicing writers, all of these form the essential core of any good graduate creative writing program. But if we want our students to succeed, we must give them more than that.

Graduate creative programs must expand to include more direct efforts to increase contacts with the publishing world, in ways that will be detailed more specifically later in this chapter. In addition, they need to continue to build on students' competencies in establishing a career in the arts, publishing or creative industries as well as enhance their opportunities to develop professionally as teachers of writing. Course *pedagogy* is perhaps less important here than in the undergraduate program, as graduate courses are by their nature less taught and the full rein of the workshop more appropriate – although more specific innovative workshop courses that recognize changes in literary culture, such as those in "the first poetry collection," might be even more useful. Moreover, additional courses themselves, in pedagogy, new media, publishing and so on, are essential.

In providing examples of the ways in which some graduate programs *are* expanding to include these elements, this chapter will spotlight some particularly effective programs and practices, as chapter two did with undergraduate programs, in the form of detailed descriptions of places where particularly exciting work is going on. The Appendix, moreover, will provide an honor roll of programs that seem to be moving in the right direction in expanding the education and services they provide to their students. The discussion in this chapter will not include low-residency or online creative writing programs, however, as these tend to cater to a different population of students, many of whom already have established primary careers. The list of ten will also leave out British programs, simply because two of the main suggestions for enhancing graduate creative writing programs emphasized in this chapter originated in the UK and are widely practiced there.

A word about publishing
It's not unusual for a student to collect her MFA and after two years of intensive study have no idea how to even format a manuscript or where to submit it for publication (Nick Mamatas, "Pulp Faction: Teaching 'Genre Fiction' in the Academy" 2008).

Whether or not students should be publishing their creative work while still in graduate school remains hotly debated. On the one side are those who feel graduate students need as much time as possible to develop their craft *outside* the exigencies of the market. Several years ago, for example, Richard Russo, a writer whose work I admire, visited our campus. After his reading, a student who was about to enter a prestigious MFA program approached him with some questions, especially about when he should try to publish. Russo asked him how long the program was. When the student replied, two years, Russo told him not to even think about publishing until near the end of his second year.

On the other side of the debate are those who feel that many students entering programs are already beginning to publish their work and that those who are not are certainly hoping to move further toward that end. Whether or not their work is "ready" varies by individual writer, however, situations such as those Nick Mamatas describes above are unjustifiable. Students can benefit from a range of publishing information and contacts that will help them when they *are* ready. This is especially true as the average age of creative writing MFA students continues to rise. With significant life and writing experience behind them, many of these older students choose MFA programs specifically because they want to learn how to publish their work. In the UK some students return for graduate degrees after they have become well published because those degrees help them find teaching jobs. At the University of Western Australia, moreover, publication of a novel or book of poems is required for entry to the postgraduate course.

One obstacle graduate programs in creative writing must attend to is a paradoxical view of the degree in the publishing world. While there is no doubt that agents and publishers recognize that such programs provide a significant majority of the next generation of successful authors, and indeed, Mark McGurl's *The Program Era* is based on the argument that the graduate writing program has been the single most influential element in American literature in the last fifty years, these same publishing professionals have also faulted such programs for not attending to the larger reading audience as they develop authors. Editorial Anonymous, a well-known publishing industry blogger and children's editor, speaks to this issue in a post that notes: "What MFA programs tend to instill in writers is an appreciation for their fellow writers as sole audience, because, through all that workshopping, your fellow writers are your sole audience ... Guess what? If you want to be published, writers are *not* your audience" (www.editorialanonymous.com 2010). Moreover, agent Donald Maass, author of *Writing the Breakout Novel*, has built a career on helping stalled writers, who may have published a successful first novel right out of the gate of their graduate programs but whose subsequent novels have failed, either to be published or to sell if they are published, because they don't really know how to write for a reader instead of other writers.

Situations such as these arise when programs are built entirely on workshops and focus solely on community. As creative writing scholar Hans Ostrom noted as late as 2010, "The old way still exists that well-known writers hired to teach undergraduate and graduate creative writing often proclaim that it can't be taught." Indeed, during the same period, Richard Bausch wrote of such programs in *The Atlantic*, "Writing is not taught in these places; it is encouraged, given room to take place and students in them always end up being better readers, whether they go on to produce books or not" (2010, p. 30). Edward Delaney addressed this problem in an earlier *Atlantic* article evaluating writing programs, where he suggested that the best writing teachers "succeed by examining what they're doing and breaking it down to its elements and really understanding the process" (Murphy Moo 2007). The best programs, I would add, are built on a philosophy that encourages the kind of teaching Delaney describes in all courses and contains mechanisms to ensure that it happens.

Beyond course content, there are other ways programs can position their students to publish their work when they *are* ready. Currently, even as the number of creative writing MFA programs increases, the ability of these programs to help their students publish varies widely. Certainly the halls of programs such as Iowa, Columbia and the University of East Anglia are well-known to be lined with agents hungry for the next big thing. The faculty at mid-list programs may be generous in introducing promising students to their own agents and editors. And hopefully, mentioning any MFA affiliation in a cover letter, indicating the serious pursuit of craft, still carries a modicum of clout, even for the graduate of the youngest programs. But there are other ways to level the playing field, if programs are serious about doing so.

Two of the most viable options, the program anthology and the publishing prize, have already become established practices in the UK, where students are forced, by the lack of assistantships and scholarships described in chapter one, to be more discriminating with their tuition dollars. That is, programs in the UK recognize that their enrollments depend on the publishing reputations of their alumni and that prospective graduate students are highly savvy about these reputations. Students in the US are becoming more savvy as well, turning frequently to blogs like Tom Kealey's *MFA Blog* and books like his *The Creative Writing MFA Handbook* – now in its second printing – to seek out the programs that are going to be most helpful to them in the long run. Social networks have developed, in fact, on the *MFA Blog* and on Seth Abramson's *The Suburban Ecstasies*, where prospective MFA students support each other, sharing program impressions, program acceptances and rejections and even "waiting list status," including such generous announcements as "I just gave up a spot at X program, so if you're on the waiting list there, you might want to contact them." What's more, these students stay in contact through these social networks after the applications season is over, providing an unprecedented cross-pollination of programs all over the world. As a result, for the first time, the world of Web 2.0 and the students who navigate it, have begun to erode the isolation and corresponding lack of transparency that has long characterized creative writing programs in higher education.

It was this lack of transparency, in fact, that nudged Tom Kealey and Seth Abramson to form these fledgling communities designed to help students compare programs. Kealey has written at length about programs internationally in *The Creative Writing MFA Handbook*. Abramson is known for his controversial efforts to rank American programs, first on his blog and later in *Poets and Writers* magazine (2009), via surveys of prospective graduate students and through an evaluation based on what those surveyed found most important, in this case: selectivity, postgraduate placement, length, funding level, cost of living and type of degree. While imperfect in some senses, as Abramson admits, and I would agree – coursework and faculty involvement, two of the most important factors through which I would evaluate a program, are noticeably absent (and indeed how can *prospective* students assess these?) – this poll nonetheless calls attention to the lack of information previously forthcoming about these programs. Prior to these, the last rankings were published in US News and World Reports in 1997 and were based on the perspectives of faculty within the programs, in a notoriously isolated system *before* the information explosion of the World Wide Web. Reports such as Kealey's and Abramson's, and my own very different assessment later in this chapter, have, despite the protestations of institutions like AWP, the critical effect of nudging programs to be more forthcoming about what their programs provide – usually on that "great equalizer" (as Abramson notes) the program website (2009, p. 84). Likewise, the need to be more forthcoming about what a program offers also has the effect of "nudging programs toward doing more for their students and encouraging all students to be more deliberate about how they make a critical life decision" (p. 91). The writing is on the wall, or the blog or the Facebook page, as it were: as students become more deliberate, programs *are* going to be held more accountable for the success of their students – they might as well begin preparing now.

Forging publishing connections

In order to stay competitive in ensuring their students achieve maximum exposure to agents and editors, most graduate writing programs in the UK have established program anthologies. Students produce a professional anthology in which each showcases an example of her work, usually selected after consulting with a faculty member. Each spring, programs launch their anthologies with a reception in the literary capital attended by editors, agents, students and faculty. In addition, following this launch, the anthology is then sent to the desks of editors and agents nationwide. Within days, Richard Kerridge, director of the Bath Spa graduate writing program, assures me, offers of publication and representation begin rolling in. As a bonus, students who work, with faculty guidance, on producing the anthology gain valuable publishing experience that gives them an edge in the literary workplace. Until recently, no US MFA programs had pursued such an anthology; however, I'm pleased to report that the University of Arizona's MFA program has recently announced the annual production of a "Look Book" that will function in the same way.

Graduate programs in the UK have also worked hard to cultivate relationships with publishers and agents via named prizes. Students attending City University London on the Creative Writing (Novels) MA course, for example, compete with one another for The Christopher Little Agency prize. Judged by the agency, winners receive a cash prize and possible representation. Moreover, judges sometimes offer representation to other entrants, who may not have won first prize but whose work they nonetheless find particularly promising. Finally, UK writing programs engage in a portfolio grading system in which student work is assessed by evaluators outside the home institution. Frequently, editors and agents are hired as outside assessors, further exposing student work to key players in the publishing world.

It would be easy to argue that such innovative approaches to forging publishing connections arise out of necessity in the UK. After all, publishing venues for short fiction are virtually nonexistent compared with the abundance of literary and little magazines available in the US which provide places for writers to publish and agents to trawl. And the US literary scene also has its share of prizes. The competition to publish in the littlest of little magazines has grown increasingly fierce, however, and the editorial response time by necessity impractically long. Through its "The Contester" column, *Poets and Writers* magazine, moreover, has reported on the rather incestuous, corrupt underbelly of many literary contests in the US, most of which carry a hefty entrance fee. The program anthology seems a much more democratic option to throw in the mix, while the agency or publisher prize, promising to bring in outside industry judges, might clear the stale air that has settled over literary awards in the US.

Certainly, these program/publishing collaborations have their drawbacks. They favor the novel or novel excerpt, for one thing, and they virtually ignore poetry, which has an altogether different market. Fortunately, the US literary landscape, in its vastness, is in a prime position to adopt these programs and modify them to fit the US publishing scene and include students of all genres.

Student-centred programs
Of the 336 (and growing) creative writing postgraduate programs in the United States, 29 have acknowledged, to greater and lesser extents, the importance of increasing the kind and diversity of curricula designed to produce savvy, successful graduates. Ten will be described here as particularly strong in this endeavor, with one MFA program, the one at the University of North Carolina Wilmington, receiving particular attention. By isolating these programs for scrutiny, I hope not only to inspire current programs to reassess the extent to which they meet the needs of today's hopeful writers but also to inspire current and future MFA students to carefully consider what they want to get out of a graduate writing program. Finally, I hope to demonstrate that it is entirely possible for an MFA program to serve more than one master – that of traditional craft – in passing the torch to the next generation of writers; that in fact, serving more than one master may ultimately result in a stronger, more sustainable literary culture. However, in end-running an obvious criticism, let me add one caveat. With the exception of the University of North Carolina Wilmington (UNCW), which has been cited by no less than *The Atlantic* magazine as an up-and-coming program, this list will have very little in common with those provided by that magazine, the *US News and World Reports, Poets and Writers* or even those

detailed in Tom Kealey's MFA guide. In fact, with the exception of my singling out of UNCW (about which I feel justified due to its acceptance by a number of other sources (AWP, *The Atlantic*) as a top program and due to its embodiment of virtually all the of qualities I was looking for), it should not be read as a ranking at all, but rather a list of programs, arranged in no particular order except to ensure topic continuity, that represent the kinds of reflective, student-centered characteristics I have been advocating throughout this book.

After a six-week study tour of programs in the UK in 2006, I returned to the US determined to look for programs that displayed the kind of foresight and focus on student preparation that I saw there, although from the beginning I was well aware that these qualities would probably take different forms in the US – and they have. My study is based on an exhaustive examination of every MFA program listed on the AWP directory up to May 2009, both the summary the program chose to list on the AWP website (telling in and of itself) and the program's website (including links to media attention, student blogs, etc.), reports from colleagues at my own institution and across the country who have attended these programs, reports from former students, information from panels on the MFA degree at the AWP conference for the past several years, and thorough research about the MFA degree program itself and the varying ways it has been interpreted at different institutions, from articles on the web and in print, blogs, and books such as *The Program Era* and *The Creative Writing MFA Handbook*. Given the vastness of the US, I did not have the resources to travel to a representative sample of the 336 programs in this country, another reason I don't feel any kind of ranking on my part would be fair. In fact, I find most rankings of this kind deeply flawed. What I aim to do here is simply describe examples of the qualities I believe are important to the twenty-first century creative writing program. I recommend that those who are faculty and administrators of such programs read these descriptions not so much to compare and find fault (as in, why aren't we serving our students in this way?) but to consider, "This is how X program is serving their students. How does our program serve ours?" Finally, I recommend that any potential or current graduate students who read this chapter regard it not so much a list of what programs to consider but of the kinds of institutional attitudes and qualities to look for in a graduate writing program.

Visionary programs
The University of Alabama at Tuscaloosa offers a number of course options beyond the traditional genre workshops, including courses in "digital media, nonfiction, screenwriting, autobiography, the profession of authorship, teaching creative writing." Tuscaloosa writing MFA students also benefit from their proximity to the MFA in the Book Arts at the School of Library and Information Studies, with all the cross-pollination that such proximity engenders. *The Black Warrior Review*, moreover, is managed entirely by graduate students, providing students with experience in literary publishing. Finally, the Tuscaloosa MFA program lists the creative-arts job placements *alongside* the prestigious publications of its graduates on its website.

The relatively new MFA in Creative Writing and the Media Arts at the *University of Missouri Kansas City* is another recent example of the ways in which a program can respond to the changing needs of literary culture by providing coursework in writing, literary publishing, broadcasting, screen and stage writing, and production skills. In addition, as part of their curriculum, students can pursue internships in a thriving Kansas City literary culture, including the literary journal *New Letters* and its sister radio program, *New Letters on the Air.*

Like several of the programs enumerated here, *Arizona State University* benefits from a close relationship with an established on-campus community literary center, in this case, the Virginia G. Piper Center for Creative Writing (profiled in detail in chapter five). Through this organization, MFA students gain community outreach experience via programs such as Young Writers at Work, and can avail themselves of the numerous authors, agents and editors streaming through the Center to give talks and classes.

The MFA Program at *Colorado State University* also provides a "variety of for-credit internships (some paid) in such areas as college teaching, public education, arts administration in literature, and literary editing (including the *Center for Literary Publishing* [and] the *Colorado Review...*)." Moreover, students can take a course in teaching college creative writing and participate in outreach programs at The Center for Community Literacy. Also in Colorado, *Naropa University's MFA program in Writing and Poetics* (residential) has carved a unique niche for itself among graduate writing programs by providing experience in letterpress printing. Like the others mentioned here, it also offers students the opportunity to become involved in literary magazine publication and outreach teaching programs. A variety of courses support this niche,

68

including Letterpress Printing, Designing A Writing Project, Translation, Project Outreach and Book Matters: An Introduction to Publishing. The last course is led by an experienced editor and includes online appearances from industry professionals.

The Chicago area (not including the Chicago Institute of Art, which will be discussed briefly in the final section of this chapter) is home to two graduate writing programs that cultivate marketable skills, along with craft, in their students. The program at *Chicago State University* requires six hours in publishing courses, including the mandatory course, Careers in Publishing. Students can also elect another fifteen hours from such courses as Writing for TV, Scriptwriting and Advanced Scriptwriting, and an internship in writing. *Roosevelt University*, moreover, offers students "multiple opportunities to prepare themselves for the working world." In addition to a growing list of courses in playwriting, screenwriting and publishing, the program also requires an internship, which can be undertaken via a number of local organizations from literary magazines to theater companies. Like a growing number of programs, moreover, Roosevelt University often funds the attendance of graduate students at the AWP annual conference.

On the West coast, *Eastern Washington University's* MFA program is designed to give students "skills and preparation for the literary job market." Home to the Inland Northwest Center for Writers, students at EWU can gain experience via courses in literary editing and design and three types of internship appointments that involve *Willow Springs*, Writers in the Community or EWU Press. Meanwhile, in the middle Atlantic, the *University of Baltimore's* MFA in Creative Writing and the Publishing Arts proclaims upfront in their program overview that "We're as concerned about what happens to you after you graduate as we are about the time you spend in our program." Indeed, not only does this program offer typical craft courses, but also courses in creativity, literary publishing, electronic publishing, creating the journal and print publishing. Beyond the typical capstone thesis of creative work, moreover, the culminating project at UB is a print or electronic publication of the student's work that he or she has written, designed and produced.

The sense of deliberateness and consideration that undergirds the MFA program at the *University of North Carolina Wilmington* is perhaps best evinced by the Department of Creative Writing's "statement of values" posted on the website – not surprisingly also the most transparent and considered site of those I studied. Prominent among Wilmington's attributes is the well-equipped Publishing Laboratory, a "classroom for graduate and undergraduate students and a fully functioning micropress," which gives students hands-on experience in the "artistic as well as the practical facts of designing, editing, and printing books." Some of the courses in the publishing laboratory include: Books and Book Publishing, Editing for Publication, Bookbuilding, and the Publishing Practicum.

The UNCW program operates with the understanding that "while short forms have their ... virtues" the central currency of the literary marketplace is the book. The curriculum is thus oriented to feature single and dual semester courses in book-length prose and poetry collections. When student work is ready, faculty members pledge to help students find agents and "place their work in appropriate venues." Finally, recognizing teaching as a "complementary and parallel art," Wilmington encourages its faculty members to be "engaged and available." Through outreach programs such as Writers in Action and the Young Writers Summer Camp, Wilmington students learn and experience the art of teaching as well as the ways in which writing teachers can become agents of social change.

Building the UNCW program
My research about the program at UNCW indicated that this relatively young program had been created with a great deal of thought and reflection. Since this book advocates such reflection more than anything else in building an effective graduate writing program, I contacted program founder and current chair Philip Gerard for an interview, in order to get a sense of how the program developed:

Did the founders of the MFA program set out specifically to create a different kind of graduate writing program? I know the program has a deeply embedded philosophy; did it have a "mission" in those early days?
Yes – everything we did was intentional. As founding director, I wrote all the documents, including the proposed curriculum, in consultation not just with our own faculty and administration but with program directors around the country. I was very active as program directors' chair and board advisor with AWP (later board member and president). So I was able to ask two crucial questions of each: What did you do right? What did you do wrong? We tried to emulate those things that worked and avoid things that sounded good until you put them into practice. So, for instance, we deliberately included Creative Nonfiction

as a track, because evidence suggested that it was a great meeting ground for poets and fiction writers, and this has proven true. We also opted for a studio-academic rather than a purely studio model, because we wanted our students to read and understand the development of the genres. Our core values always included genre-crossing, partly because all our faculty have worked in multiple genres, and we always keep that in mind whenever we hire. On the other hand, we decided against a thesis option in screenwriting, even though we have faculty who teach courses in it, because we really couldn't cover it effectively or thoroughly. We also don't teach courses in writing for children or YA. In other words, figure out what you do well, and do those things. Don't try to be all things to all people. We also conducted a feasibility study, gave questionnaires to current and former students, closely examined successful programs that like us were started recently in resort locations, and in general did unusually thorough due diligence, including projections of how many students we wanted each year, building to an optimum number. As one of our new sub-deans recently said, "You guys actually have a business plan." We make good plans, then we live by them. We always design courses with this in mind: What course did WE want as students?

How did the idea to start the Publishing Laboratory come about? How was it realized?

Stanley Colbert and his wife Nancy, both formerly literary agents and publishers running HarperCollins Canada, arrived one day in the area after retiring from successful careers and wanted to contribute. So he taught a course called "Getting Published," – tremendously popular. He split his students into teams and had them bid on imaginary books he dreamed up. Each team had a budget. It had to buy the book and make a P&L statement, figure out a print run, etc. He also taught query letters, agenting, etc. Gradually this grew into this concept that he could show students how to actually make a book –not just conceptually but physically. So in a closet-sized space with a couple of old computers, his gang began designing a textbook for our intro class (which has a master instructor and many graduate teaching assistants and was designed as a way of both introducing undergraduates to the discipline and providing an interesting teaching experience for our GTAs beyond freshman comp[osition]). We were championed by a great dean and a great chancellor, both of whom supported our move to become an independent department. The dean subsequently found us an old building and we got bond money to renovate it – now we have a great home and were able to design in a state-of-the-art publishing laboratory upstairs and support it. Our current dean was keen to see all departments set up an applied learning experience, and this was a perfect venue. All our undergrad seniors do a publishing project – either an independent chapbook or a class anthology – supervised by Emily Smith and her specially trained GTA staff in the lab.

The program seems to spin out from a center in several directions – I'm thinking of the Publishing Laboratory, the outreach to schools, the journal Ecotone, *the press, the international exchanges – what is the program's (and your) secret to keeping so many initiatives going?*

Our departmental governance is simple but crucial. We have coordinators for each degree, BFA and MFA, who recommend policy and scheduling and keep tabs on all the day-to-day stuff, such as training, morale, etc. Our Publishing Lab director does the same thing for her shop. Our BFA coordinator doubles as outreach coordinator and supervises those very amazing student leaders. Ben George does *Ecotone*. All are topnotch and experienced professionals. I let them really run their areas, but I will not hesitate to step in and back them up or take something off their desk if they are overwhelmed. We meet weekly to discuss anything happening in their areas. For instance, MFA admissions is a huge process and everyone is involved. BFA admissions ditto. We need to coordinate training of GTAs, who teach in the BFA program but of course are MFA students. My job is to set a tone, act as ringmaster, make sure the very complicated budget gets done, work with deans, provost, and chancellor on a variety of long-term planning issues and with Advancement on fundraising, and ultimately be the authority when somebody has to say yes or no. I advocate for my department within the university, do my best to enhance its reputation beyond, and also persuade faculty to serve in the various roles. Two important things: We all get along very well, and our students are pretty wonderful and step up in terrific ways; and second, we try to create policy independent of personalities. That is, imagine everybody currently affected by it will be gone – will it be a wise and useful policy in that case? Your analogy of the hub is accurate. The two academic programs are the core, but they intersect in all the other areas. As chair, I am the responsible central authority for hiring, spending money, implementing policy, and making faculty assignments in and out of the classroom, but I rely on a lot of other people, including two excellent administrative staff. The coordinators rely on faculty committees, whose role is to actually do work on behalf of the programs – such as assessment, ranking for admissions, etc., rather than merely offer guidance. Everybody is involved at some level – even our very active graduate student association has a rep on our MFA committee and has regularly brought suggestions for new courses, new policy, etc., and we have responded.

The faculty – including yourself – are obviously productive and well published, yet their energy and involvement is essential to the program. How does the UNCW MFA balance the faculty's need to foster their own work and careers with the demands of teaching and mentoring students? Do you have a guiding principle here?

Everybody writes. Everybody teaches. We value the time in the classroom and make it clear to students at all levels that that enthusiasm is fueled by our time at the writing desk. Our faculty also are quite successful at winning competitive research reassignments (no teaching for a semester) and outside grants to give them a breather from teaching in order to tackle long projects. And more senior faculty such as Clyde Edgerton and Phil Furia have routinely mentored less senior faculty in helping to place work or to revise it.

Accolades for the program have been piling up for the first ten years – recognition from The Atlantic, *AWP and so on – as the UNCW MFA has established itself as a visionary program on the American literary scene. What's in store for the next ten?*

The Publishing Laboratory is an area of growth, especially as Emily and her crew start to plan for the age beyond print. They already are doing lots of online and digital stuff, so now it's a question of where the book as art fits in. It's actually an exciting, if nail-biting, time. As for curriculum, we have one that works and now it's a matter of tweaking. But we're also launching our new strategic planning season this fall with a retreat, so we'll see where we think we are and what we have to do to remain nimble and innovative.

I hope it doesn't sound like I'm bragging, but in truth something pretty special is going on here, and in some sense my job now is not to mess it up. Mark Cox, our founding chair, imprinted his strong ethic of community spirit and professional generosity on the department, and Phil Furia continued that work. I have two excellent former chairs to rely on for thorny issues, and a wealth of institutional knowledge among the faculty and staff.

One last thing. Whenever we welcome our new MFA students, we ask them, "What will you contribute to the program? What will be your legacy?" They are here not just to benefit from their time in the program but to give back – to it and the profession. And their legacies have been memorable.

Fine arts institutes and special programs

MFA programs housed in art institutes, such as those at the *Art Institute of Chicago*, the *California College of the Arts*, and the *Otis School of Art and Design*, deserve mention for an often innovative, interdisciplinary approach to curriculum design that takes into account new media, genre writing (comics and graphic novels, for example) and publishing. These are worth consideration for anyone working in those genres and provide models for other MFA programs in creating courses outside the traditional four genre box (fiction, poetry, creative nonfiction and drama). The international MFA program at the *University of Nevada at Las Vegas*, moreover, features a "Peace Corps Track," which offers young poets and fiction writers an option that enables them to meet the obligations of the program, become bilingual and serve the current needs of the third world.

It goes without saying that these kinds of programs require at least an initial infusion of capital (the Look Book at the University of Arizona, for example, is underwritten by one outside donor). It also goes without saying that the MFA in Creative Writing can be a major cash cow for any institution that houses it. Faced with a glut of creative writing programs, however, it is only a matter of time before potential students start voting with their feet, and the herd begins to starve. That's the bad news. The good news is that, given the emergence of these innovative programs, it is easy to dream of a creative writing landscape in America where there's room for people at different stages along the continuum of writing development, where schools tilt toward giving students an abundance of tools to sustain themselves after they graduate, and where these programs join with other initiatives, such as the community based programs described in chapter five, to form the foundation of a rebirth of literary culture in America.

Notes from the Field
Once More to the Workshop:
A Myth Caught in Time

> This seemed an utterly enchanted sea, this lake you could leave to its own devices for a few hours and come back to, and find that it had not stirred, this constant and trustworthy body of water.
>
> (*"Once More to the Lake"* E. B. White, 1941)

In his famous, canonized essay *"Once More to the Lake,"* E.B. White elegizes the lake he visited with his family as a boy, the same one to which he, now a father, brings his son, romanticizing this place of memory until it is utterly frozen in time, an idealized icon. In much the same way, the traditional writing workshop, alternately a site of criticism and rosy nostalgia, has suffered the same fate.

The problem with icons is that they are static; unable, from their fragile pedestals, to respond to sea changes that surround them, to evolve and remain relevant to the society in which they were anointed. Pictures of Elvis, Marilyn Monroe, even Mickey Mouse, dominate our visual memories just like the idyllic lake White romanticizes, but they are dead images, their relevance to society buried at the moment they ceased to grow and change with the rest of the world. If the creative writing workshop is to survive and retain its efficacy, it must resist this iconic tendency and respond to the educational landscape in which it currently exists instead of the one in which it was conceived over half a century ago. It must be revised.

Some of the other campers were in swimming ... one of them
with a cake of soap. Over the years there has been this person
with the cake of soap, this cultist, and here he was. There had
been no years.

Famously implemented at the University of Iowa through
the vision of Norman Foerster and later Paul Engle, the
workshop's primary intention was to provide a post-
baccalaureate incubator where "young *polished* [emphasis
mine] writers could come for a year or two and have their
work critiqued" (Swander 2005, p. 168). Forester and
Engle also constructed the workshop as a place where these
"seasoned" writers could be hardened to the critics, where
success could be claimed if a student (usually a female)
occasionally and perhaps apocryphally (for we know writers
are great storytellers) fainted after a particularly rigorous
session. A place, Tom Grimes fondly muses, whose entrance
should be guarded by the signage, "Abandon all hope, all ye
who enter here," (Grimes qted. in Wandor 2008, p. 131).

Known in some circles as the Bobby Knight school of
writing pedagogy, so named for the famously abusive,
chair-throwing American college basketball coach, the
workshop was also designed as a kind of "boot camp"
which would "toughen" students so that they could
withstand inevitable adversity and criticism as an artist
(Swander 2005, p. 168). Such goals are not surprising, for
contributing to the uniqueness of the workshop's origins
was the fact that at mid-century, most of the students in
the eponymous Iowa Workshop were males, many of them
Second World War veterans on the GI bill, for whom the
humiliations of boot camp and varnished floors of the
basketball court were easily internalized metaphors.

And internalize them they did, as these young writers fanned out to become writing teachers themselves and modeled their own workshops on the only method of teaching they had known, so that the abusive basketball coach school of pedagogy dominated the creative writing scene for many years and still counts a number of enthusiasts today. As Swander notes, "Every creative writing instructor must face the Bobby Knight legacy" (2005, p. 169). Indeed, many teachers feel they must still aspire to it, as evident when teacher Dan Barden congratulates himself, in a recent article on his workshop teaching in *Poets and Writers* magazine, on the fact that "one of the things that makes me a good teacher, I'm convinced, is that I'm a bastard" (2008, p. 87).

> On the journey to the lake, I began to wonder what it would be like. I wondered how time would have marred this unique, this holy spot.

The essential problem with this method of pedagogy arises in the ways in which the creative writing landscape has changed since the early days of the Iowa workshop. With the exception of postgraduate programs, the overwhelming majority of creative writing workshop students bear no resemblance to the cadre of graduate students, the "polished" writers who populated the workshop as it took hold in creative writing mythology. Teacher and writer Brent Royster recognizes this when he cautions that "creative writing workshops are growing in popularity" to the extent that a "revised notion of creativity and a restructuring," becomes necessary (2005, p. 35).

Mary Swander notes, as well, that "when creative writing became democratized," that is, as hundreds of creative writing programs, both graduate and undergraduate, sprang up in the last fifty years, the student population changed. "Poetry, fiction and playwriting [were] offered to students with little *developed* [emphasis mine] literary skill" (2005, p. 168). Moreover, as creative writing programs trickled or gushed down to the undergraduate level, the face of the creative writing classroom changed from the rarefied countenances of more experienced writers to the wide-eyed stares of absolute beginners who felt called to write but who had no idea what this calling entailed, having, for the most part, cultivated their passion for writing outside a classroom (high school creative writing courses are still unusual except in larger or more affluent secondary schools), yet still inside a popular culture that perpetuated, and continues to perpetuate, a laundry list of myths about how writers and writing come to be. The Bobby Knight school of teaching creative writing, in which students learn to write in an economy of scarcity, where the only guidance centers on what *not* to do, ultimately fails beginning writers. Even Barden seems to recognize this as he bemoans the inefficacy of the workshop in educating his undergraduate writers, but nonetheless, as we have seen, clings to the Romantic myth, as to a life raft, that in order to be a "good" workshop leader he must maintain his reputation as a "bastard."

There was a choice of pie for dessert and the waitresses were the same country girls ... still fifteen; their hair had been washed, that was the only difference – they had been to the movies and seen the pretty girls with the clean hair.

81

The necessity of retrofitting the workshop for changing populations, especially for undergraduates, is perhaps best illustrated in the story Swander tells of her first, undergraduate experience of the iconic "workshop": "Write a story for next week," the instructor told them.

"But isn't she going to show us how to write a short story?" the young Swander wonders. "There must be parts, components, to a short story, different styles and structures. Is she even going to explain the choices we could make?" (2005, p. 167).

In fact, the traditional, product-centered creative writing workshop gives little to no attention to invention and creativity, to how poems, short stories, essays or plays are actually *constructed*. To this end, Barden characterizes the workshop as "anything *but* a shop in which writers work," (p. 83). Such workshops, moreover, as Royster maintains, lose sight of their real goal, to scaffold or "foster more dedicated writers" (p. 27).

Michelene Wandor, in her discussion of the traditional workshop in her book, *The Writer is Not Dead, Merely Somewhere Else*, also notes the paradox that arises in a beginning writing class when "workshop time (the foregrounded activity) is reserved for student writing ... completed *outside* of class [emphasis mine]. Even if the student thinks it's complete, the fact that it is subject to group criticism renders it conceptually incomplete" (2008, p. 127). Royster underscores another paradox when he refers to the long held workshop wisdom that the student whose work is "on the table," must be silent when it is under discussion: "the work of the class is the daily practice of writing and the shared process of that practice," and yet, in the unadulterated workshop, students may be cautioned "in speaking about their process in favor of listening to peer criticism" (p. 34).

The answer to this workshop dilemma seems relatively clear and yet, perhaps because many creative writing teachers *still* do not avail themselves of the growing body of scholarship on the teaching of creative writing characterized by this book and many, many others (Barden's essay, for example, demonstrates no awareness of this scholarship), it continues to elude them. Simply put, the workshop must be modified to respond to the varying populations of students who wish – and deserve – to benefit from it. Critically, the workshop for beginning writers, usually undergraduates, must be refocused to include content that enhances skill building and craft.

Indeed, Barden is right when he worries that the "root of the problem is that the way we teach creative writing ... suggests that there is *no way to teach creative writing*" (p. 83). Even as a "naïve" undergraduate, Swander observed that in other skill-building classes, "students were asked to practice the basic steps of the craft, carefully mastering a chunk of knowledge before adding another" (p. 167). Wandor, further holds up as an example the Italian Renaissance art academies where more "formal ways of teaching fine art developed ... anatomy, life drawing, natural philosophy, and architecture were all part of the curriculum ...the idea was to get away from the empirical haphazard kind of learning that artists had faced in workshops" (p. 132).

Sound familiar? In order to succeed in the current terrain, the traditional workshop must, as all writers-in-training are exhorted to do, *respond* to its audience. Workshops whose students are at the start of the continuum of their development as writers must first of all de-emphasize the *shop* (defined by Royster as the "daily critique that underscores the weakness in the writer's work") in favor of the work – the aforementioned "daily practice of writing and the shared process of that practice."

Such a reinvention can take any number of forms, including de-mystifying the writer's life and creative practice – my own introductory classes always include writers' memoirs through which students will learn that there is no one kind of writing practice any more than there is one kind of writer. It is also heavily exercise-based; students do as much writing inside the class as outside of it. Beginning writers especially, need to know that writing doesn't spring fully formed from their pens and laptops but is the result of recursive drafting, self-assigned creativity exercises and the like. Finally, it may include substantial reflection on individual process, so that students may discover the creative practices that most support and enhance their development as writers. All of these conditions recreate what Wendy Bishop termed the "transactional" creative writing workshop, one that puts "writers in motion" (1998, p. 14). Moreover, in the hands of those for whom creativity is second nature, reinventing the traditional workshop may ultimately result in inventive forms of teaching we have not even discovered yet, once the necessity of this reinvention is understood as a given in the field.

Throughout "Once More to the Lake," E.B. White describes the lake as so frozen in time that he has trouble "making out which was I, the one walking at my side, [or] the one walking in my pants." At the end of the essay, moreover, he watches, a late-middle-aged spectator, as his son prepares to swim after a heavy storm. As "[his son] buckle[s] the swollen belt," of his swimsuit, White's groin suddenly feels the "chill of death."

At a 2008 Association of Writers and Writing Programs Conference craft lecture, fiction writer Joan Silber said, "A story is the rescuer of time like fish from a moving stream." Unlike E. B. White's intimations of mortality, the death of the workshop is not a foregone conclusion. It can be rescued from the moving stream that threatens to carry it into iconoclastic oblivion, and re-cast, recreated into something lithe and supple. Our students deserve no less.

Chapter Four

Workshopping the Workshop

If creative writing in higher education in the past few decades, for reasons warranted and unwarranted, has become a popular target of cultural criticism, the workshop itself sits at the bull's-eye of that criticism. For some time now, "to say that a book smacks of the creative writing workshop has become a sort of reviewer's cliché, a shorthand...for the idea that the work in question is trite" (Madison Smartt Bell qtd. in Leahy 2010, p. 64). According to D.G. Myers, the term workshop first entered the American-English lexicon in the late nineteenth-century, characterizing drama classes at Harvard that were designed to "shorten a little the time of the writer's apprenticeship," (qtd. in Mayers 2005, p. 67) a definition that may be most remarkable for the fact that it has changed so little in the last hundred years.

Indeed, as Dianne Donnelly points out in the introduction to her edited collection *Does the Writing Workshop Still Work?*, when one speaks of the pedagogy … of creative writing, the workshop is implied in the address" (2010, p. 5). In the same volume, Anna Leahy extends this definition by asserting that if creative writing is to be considered a profession like law or medicine, it must also have a "signature pedagogy and that signature pedagogy is the workshop" (2010, p. 65). Perhaps the best way to examine the current conflicted state of this signature pedagogy is to subject it to a similar form of classroom evaluation: let's workshop the workshop.

What's working in the workshop

To begin, we'll follow the customary workshop rule that praise should precede criticism. It is important to note, then, that there are reasons why the workshop is so well suited to the teaching of creative writing, reasons that explain its exceptional endurance. Citing creativity studies, and echoing a refrain introduced in earlier chapters of this book, Leahy notes that "community," a feature of virtually any workshop, "is often especially important for creative production" (p. 67). She elaborates, moreover, that five conditions must exist "to produce a cultural environment that nurtures creativity: intellectual freedom, other creative people, a fair but competitive atmosphere, mentors and supporters, and economic prosperity" (p. 68). Certainly, the creative writing workshop meets all of these conditions, even, she points out, economic prosperity, in the form of the financial buffer that higher education institutions provide from the vagaries of the publishing industry: university workshops continue in times both fecund and fallow.

Philip Gross extends this praise by extolling the workshop as a sacred space that "continues the developmental business begun in childhood where wide possibilities (some of them risky or absurd) get tested with thought and imagination, within boundaries" (2010, p. 61). As a progressive educational model, moreover, it is distinguished by the "belief that each and every person's contribution will be part of the learning experience for everybody else" (p. 56). In order to remain a progressive educational model, however, the workshop must not remain static. So that we can keep what is the heart of the workshop, what *is* effective about this space, so well enumerated by Leahy,

Gross and others, we must continually examine the water that surrounds it, filtering out, if you will, what doesn't work, especially those practices which no longer function effectively because they are outmoded and fail to support the current, diverse generations of students who are at its center.

Before we begin "filtering," however, it's worth considering that part of the workshop's "identity problem" is just that, an identity problem. Years ago, American writer Philip Roth famously described the "Three Objectives" of the workshop as to give young writers: i.) an audience; ii.) a sense of community; iii.) an acceptable social category, that of student (qtd. in Grimes 1999 pp. 4–5). Certainly the first two can and have been repeatedly linked to heightening artistic development. The last, however, simply adds to the sense that the workshop is really just a "front" for students who want to prolong their sense of themselves as artists in the face of parental pressure. All three objectives, moreover, are just vague enough to ensure that in claiming to be all things to all writers, the workshop might not actually serve any of them well. According to Paul Dawson, the workshop can be a mysterious place where "the pedagogical process is merely guided by the idiosyncrasies of each teacher, the practicing writer able to pass on knowledge by virtue of his or her innate talent and secret knowledge of the craft" (2005, p.1). Dianne Donnelly further problematizes the "melting pot" approach to the workshop "as a little of this and a lot of that, a community crock pot of flavors," entirely dependent on the workshop leader and the participants when she laments that "it is no wonder that at times, we are unsure of just what it is we taste in this covered dish, this workshop. And we wonder how it might sustain us" (2010, p. 8). Should we call for more uniformity, more prescribed rigor in the writing workshop then? Such a solution hardly seems possible or preferable given the range of students the workshop serves, as well as the range of teachers who teach it and genres they teach. I would argue a little identity problem can be a good thing. It can keep us on our toes, as we wonder what is this thing called the workshop and, more critically, as Donnelly aptly asks, how might it sustain us? The answer to this question, I believe, lies in constant interrogation, in asking over and over, "how might it *best* sustain us?" – an interrogation that requires that we keep workshopping the workshop. Without further ado.

What's not working in the workshop

Now, the criticism, or what's "not working" in the workshop. A review of the scholarship indicates that the list is a long one, which perhaps can best be introduced by a vignette that appears in the "Workshop" chapter of Tom Kealey's *The Creative Writing MFA Handbook*: "When you're a writer in workshop, it's like driving a car with twelve people in the backseat, all of them telling you which way to go. They all may actually be giving good directions and driving instructions but if you listen to all of them, you're likely to crash the car" (2008, p. 175). Undeniably, many critics trace the problems in the workshop back to the overwhelming number of cooks spoiling the soup, underscoring the complaint that the course evinces a kind of "creativity by committee," where instead of setting out to become "great writers with a wide audience," students are eventually trained to recast their sights on pleasing the audience in the immediate classroom (Mayers 2010, p. 96). Further, by reducing the participant's aspirations to pleasing the workshop audience, including the teacher, the workshop courts a number of other flaws enumerated in Starkey and Bishop's *Keywords in Creative Writing*, such as "punishing risk-taking and rewarding uniformity," "silencing the author during the discussion of her own work, [thereby] destabilizing the necessarily dialogic nature of the writing process," "creating a harrowing experience for the writer," and, finally (whew!) "giving short shrift to the invention exercises ... writers need to generate writing" (Starkey 2006, p. 121). Adding to this list, Kass Fleisher maintains, in "Scenes from the Battlefield: A Feminist Resists the Writing Workshop," that the workshop model "actively suppresses both feminist radical writing and avant garde writing," instead perpetuating "the status quo" (2002, p. 109). Finally, Sue Roe points out that "for aspiring students full of ideas but as yet unversed in the need to learn technique, there may be a temptation to see peer discussion and feedback as fundamental, the rest (learning technique, reading comparable works, pursuing related research) as [merely] the academic padding" (2010, p. 199).

Suggestions for improvement

Given this laundry list of concerns, the "author" presenting the "workshop" for workshopping would probably be pretty despondent by now. Such despondence traditionally undergirds another common workshop practice: workshop criticism is most effective when coupled with *suggestions* for helping the author realize his vision. Tim Mayers, for example, writes that "the workshop's greatest strength

– that it provides apprentice writers with a responsive audience, becomes ironically its greatest weakness," as its participants become "estranged from the real audience," (a criticism also leveled at workshops by the publishing industry as noted in chapter three) (2010, pp. 96–97). He accompanies this criticism with some considered suggestions, however.

At the heart of the workshop, Mayers suggests, is fundamentally the way we teach writers to consider real or potential audiences and "to put that thinking into action in their own writing processes" (p. 94). After much reflection, Mayers finds the "question of which audience a text seems to *invoke* is a profitable one in workshops" (p. 103). In doing so, he borrows a concept from Composition Studies – Lunsford and Ede's "audience addressed and audience invoked." According to Lunsford and Ede, writing is usually either "audience addressed" or pitched toward real-life people who are reading a discourse (e.g. an essay on natural pesticides for *Organic Gardening* magazine), or "audience invoked," that is, called up or invented by the writer" (e.g. a hard-boiled detective story presumes an audience who enjoys mysteries) (p. 101). After introducing these terms in his creative writing workshops, Mayers is able to fluidly discuss notions of audience in effective ways, such as the time he asked a student who had included an extensive, painstakingly accurate description of fingerprinting technique in a story, what audience he was "invoking?" Was the student writing for detectives who would be familiar with the process (the student had interviewed some) or a more general readership? The student allowed that he was actually seeking a more general readership, which led to a fruitful class discussion as to whether the subtleties of fingerprinting might not be as important to a wider audience. By foregrounding the workshop with such technical terms as "audience addressed" and "audience invoked," Mayers was able to raise the stakes and the learning experience for all involved. By enlarging the discussion of audience he is also able to address the criticism that workshop writers learn to write "only for one another."

Kevin Brophy worries that the workshop "dominates a creative writing semester's class time so much that what a student learns most effectively might be how to cope with the workshop as a ritual, as a contest" (2008, p. 80). He had also observed, however, that students often hungered for more feedback on their work, perhaps naturally so since one student might only receive feedback on her work twice in the duration of his traditional workshop. To address this hunger and to realign the course from mere survival of a ritual, he decided to create many more opportunities for feedback and vary the methods by which the students received it. Beyond the two full-class workshops, his students now have the opportunity to share their work in small groups, in online spaces and in a public class reading. I have made similar changes to my own workshops; increasing the number of pieces that I comment on and integrating an online community in which work is shared, as well as ending with a sharing of the "chapbooks" my students create at the close of the semester. Much like the end of course portfolio, only typically more visually refined and appealing, individual chapbooks are celebrated with a launch party, at which each student is given a stack of small post-it notes and the class exchanges chapbooks. For two hours, students read each other's work in hushed wonder and each student brings home a chapbook interleaved with a countless yellow slips of (removable) feedback.

Philip Gross sees the workshop as evolving over the course of the three-year undergraduate British creative writing curriculum, "with instruction leading towards self-reliance" (2010, p. 59). In the first year, students would learn "the process and some trust," while in year two they would be encouraged to "experiment...under close guidance," and in year three, they would be "confident and skilled enough for the workshopping of works-in-progress" to be their main vehicle for improvement (p.59). Ultimately, students would graduate with those skills integrated so that they could be reproduced and applied elsewhere (p. 59). It is easy to see how such a graduated plan of study could be adapted for other curricular structures, such as those in the US.

David Starkey, who teaches at Santa Barbara City College, a two-year institution, contends that the workshop method is particularly ill-suited to the two-year college for a number of reasons related to student preparedness, low student retention and student distraction. In other words, it is difficult to build community in a several weeks workshop when student attendance is spotty, their literary background is uneven at best and they are struggling to meet a wider range of basic economic survival needs. For the workshop to succeed in such circumstances, he notes, "it must be only *one* [emphasis mine] component of a multifaceted approach to teaching creative writing" (p. 151). In addition to the challenges of teaching this specific subgroup, two-year college students might also be considered "uber-undergraduates" then, who require a much more taught workshop. While it may be easy to dismiss this population as entirely too narrow when reconsidering the pedagogy of the workshop, Starkey is quick to point out that as the job market for creative writing teachers becomes increasingly competitive, many will find themselves in institutions teaching just this group.

So far our examination of the workshop has centered on the undergraduate workshop. What of the graduate workshop? Certainly the undergraduate and graduate workshops can be said to serve different masters – the former a more diverse population, the latter a self-selected group of more experienced writers. Does this circumstance relieve the graduate workshop of the same burden of reflection, of asking again how this creative writing institution might best sustain and develop the next generation? Hardly. Instead, we might reflect once more, as Donnelly reminds us, on the gains to be made by "flexing the elasticity of the workshop model" (2010, p. 19).

Horror stories from graduate workshops continue to abound, of famous teachers who appear once a week for a three-hour class to facilitate discussion of a work they have not read, to read their weekly mail aloud, at the worst, or, at best, to reinscribe the status quo at the expense of more experimental writing, to confirm what the community of writers already knows (Starkey 2010). "That was then," some might say, "this is now. The workshop has changed, evolved, become more accountable to its constituents." Donnelly finds evidence of this change in the rise in "digital writing workshops ... teaching with wikis, blogs, and moodle ..." (2010, p. 24). However, she also reminds us that we must continue to ask, "What else is possible in the [graduate] creative writing workshop-based classroom?" (p. 24).

Because undergraduate creative writing is more taught, the population more diverse, one might say that those who teach in it predominantly might be forced to be more creative, reflective in teaching it, more likely to turn, as Tim Mayers and David Starkey and many others did, to the "scholarship" of creative writing pedagogy in determining how best to teach this group of nascent writers. A quick mental survey of those who are currently "writing" the scholarship of the workshop reveals that the majority teach undergraduate creative writing, occasionally a mix of graduate and undergraduates. How to convince graduate programs, then, and graduate professors, of the need to keep the workshop vigorous, to make it new, to stay abreast of current workshop theory and practice in journals such as *TEXT, New Writing: An International Journal of Creative Writing Theory and Practice,* and the English Subject Centre's cwteaching.co.uk?

One way is to raise the bar in teaching undergraduates, thus raising their expectations of what a workshop can be. Graduate students who have experienced more reflective, responsive programs with maximally involved faculty, who have been taught as undergraduates to look critically not only at their classmates' work, but also at their own work and the workshop itself, tend to be more savvy, reflective members of the graduate workshop. My experience teaching mostly undergraduates, who often remain in contact with me once they join graduate programs, tells me that this is true, as does the experience of my colleagues both at my own institution and others. More sophisticated students are less likely to be tolerant of a minimally involved professor or a decades old workshop model, and more likely to demand better teaching and to flock toward those who provide it; while those who do not, we can hope, preside over smaller and smaller classes as they slouch toward retirement.

Other ways are more complicated. Certainly, we can hope that more and more teachers of graduate creative writing avail themselves of the pedagogy of the field while at the same time probe their own creative faculties in building a better workshop. Changes in the AWP conference in the past few years seem to indicate a shift, small but significant nonetheless, toward more substantive pedagogy sessions and discussions about the graduate workshop. Moreover, the 20 programs listed in chapter three and the Appendix represent places where the graduate workshop has not persisted as a static artifact, but thrived as a living, developing being. Importantly, a growing number of these programs also feature courses in the teaching of creative writing, a development I would argue is essential to the future survival of creative writing in higher education. For it is here, in these courses, where the viability of this signature pedagogy is questioned and where students who plan to go out and teach it can be encouraged to view it not as a static icon but instead as an evolving entity that deserves their full attention. It is here, in these courses, that the next generation of writers will be taught how to teach and encouraged to reflect on their practice and eventually, on the programs they will be charged to lead. In "Professional Writers/Writing Professionals: Revamping Teacher Training in Creative Writing Ph.D. Programs," published in *College English* in 2001, Kelly Ritter lamented the lack of training for graduate students in the teaching of writing. Nine years later, there are at least 30 creative writing pedagogy courses in graduate programs in the

United States alone. So long as this number continues to rise, and these courses are made available to those who confess a desire to become publishing writers who also teach, the future of the creative writing workshop looks promising indeed.

Notes from the Field

A Place to Start: A Brief Narrative Bibliography of Creative Writing Theory and Pedagogy

The last time I saw Wendy Bishop was in February 2003 at the AWP Conference in Baltimore. It was the eve of the Iraq war. As we drove into the city at dusk, I remember making urgent anti-war cell phone calls to my congressman. Fred Rogers, the gentle television icon of many an American childhood, had just died and though we had no way of knowing it then, Wendy Bishop herself would be leaving us – far, far too prematurely – before the year was out.

That day, she told the audience that it was the first time she'd been back to AWP in a while, though she'd been on the Board for some years in the early 90s. Bishop and her friend and frequent collaborator Kate Haake were together on a panel taking stock of creative writing theory and pedagogy: where it had been and where it was going. Central to Wendy's message was that, for all the strides that had been made, creative writing pedagogy would never fully arrive as a discipline until there was a central depository, a bibliography, if you will, of the growing number of books and articles that wrestled with the essential issues of theory and practice. Until then, writers wishing to engage in discourse about their field would have to proceed, hit or miss, through Google searches (Google Scholar had not yet been established) and ERIC (Education Resources Information Center) databases, hoping to find the background they needed. Until then, some teacher-writers would continue writing articles questioning the value of the workshop or musing whether, indeed, creative writing could be taught, as if these questions had never been raised before. Over and over, in isolation and on different continents, creative writers and teachers would exhaust themselves reinventing that wheel.

Certainly, during that cold, gray Saturday afternoon, Wendy was preaching to the choir. Silently, we nodded in our seats, turned to our neighbors, whispered, "Right. Yes. Absolutely. Needs to be done."

But none of us took up the cause. Despite their necessity, bibliographies are hard work and not intellectually glamorous work at that. And so, six years later, the literature review in creative writing pedagogy essays often remains spotty, and very occasionally, doesn't exist at all. Creative writers still commiserate, as they did this past February at AWP in Chicago, on whether discussions of the utility of the workshop and its alternatives might be growing a bit repetitive, that it might be time to move the conversation forward.

Steve Healey at once tells us that "what has been missing from the impressive success story of creative writing is an equally strong attention to its pedagogy and theory ..." (2009, p. 30) and then acknowledges that some "ground clearing has been done in the growth of a nascent body of reflexive criticism about creative writing" (p.38). This characterization of creative writing, while accurate on some levels, is distinctive for what it leaves out. Nascent, in fact, implies something that is "just beginning to develop, to grow, to come into existence" (www.dictionary.com). Rather, I would argue that Healey's essay begins, as most good narratives do, in media res, after much work *has* been done reflecting on creative writing theory and pedagogy. Unfortunately, long after Wendy Bishop issued her call to action, the problem remains that little has been done to document this work in a central location, to tell the *story* of the growth of creative writing theory and practice, one that begins as early as 1989 with Joseph Moxley's *Creative Writing in America* and proceeds, in fits and starts, through the 1990s, reaching a groundswell in the early part of this century.

I am still not much of a bibliographer, but I am a storyteller and this is one story I feel compelled and qualified to tell, since, along with many of my mentors and colleagues, I am part of it. In doing so, I hope to provide a brief narrative bibliography of the last twenty years of our discipline, so that current and future writers and scholars will have key resources to consider when contextualizing their own work in our growing field.

Indeed, beginning with Moxley's *Creative Writing in America*, Creative Writing as a discipline might have been most accurately described as "nascent" during the 1990s, when a handful of figures gathered to light the fire that would become the discipline and labored to keep it burning. Wendy Bishop, of course, was a major figure during this period, along with her frequent collaborators, Katharine Haake, Hans Ostrom and David Starkey. Any thorough reflection on aspects of the field as a whole requires an understanding of their pioneering work in *Colors of a Different Horse: Rethinking Creative Writing Theory and Pedagogy*, (Bishop, Haake, Ostrom), *Released Into Language: Options for Teaching Creative Writing* (Bishop), *What Our Speech Disrupts: Feminism and Creative Writing Studies* (Haake) and *Teaching Writing Creatively* (Starkey). D.W. Fenza's apologias and brief histories of the field in *The Writer's Chronicle* are also crucial to this period. D.G. Myer's *The Elephants Teach: Creative Writing Since 1880* (reprinted in 2006), Patrick Bizzaro's *Responding to Student Poems: Applications of Critical Theory* and Mary Ann Cain's *Revisioning Writers' Talk: Gender and Culture in Acts of Composing*, as well as the founding of the Australian online international creative writing and teaching journal *TEXT* in 1997 (http://www.textjournal.com.au/), round out the important work of the decade.

Another indicator that Creative Writing was truly maturing as a discipline was the 2004 launch of *New Writing: An International Journal of Theory and Practice* in the UK by Multilingual Matters. Founded and still edited by Graeme Harper, a prolific writer and scholar and familiar face at American and British creative writing conferences, *New Writing* provided creative writers a dedicated forum in which to regularly debate the issues of pedagogy and theory. Five years later, the journal remains strong. Now published by Taylor & Francis, it has moved from two issues a year to three, including an index issue that is already proving valuable to the field.

The early part of this century not only saw a continued uptick in scholarly activity from the players who had initiated the conversation, as noted earlier, but also included a few new team members such as Kelly Ritter and Shirley Geoklin Lim, as well as several whose work will be described below. In addition, the fruits of two intense scholarly labors debuted in 2005, Australian author Paul Dawson's *Creative Writing and the New Humanities* and Tim Mayers' *(Re)Writing Craft: Composition, Creative Writing and the Future of English Studies*. Both landmark books, Dawson's examines the issues surrounding the multi-continental birth and growth of Creative Writing in higher education in the US, the UK and Australia and considers the unique contexts that gave rise to each of them. Mayers examines the histories of Composition Studies and Creative Writing Studies as sub fields within English Studies in the US and proposes an alliance between them, a space "in which collaboration might occur...an area of common concern that might be called Writing Studies" (p. 167). Following on the heels of these two singly authored volumes would be Anna Leahy's *Power and Identity in the Creative Writing Classroom: The Authority Project*, an impressive collection of seventeen essays by new and established voices that re-examine "prevalent assumptions about workshops and other common practices in order to both understand and revise them," and help provide "a unified approach for those entering and continuing to teach in the field" (p. ix). A year later, Graeme Harper published another collection, *Teaching Creative Writing*, whose chapters are broken down by subject (e.g. workshopping) and genre (teaching the short story) in order to provide resources for teachers creating and/or reflecting upon their own pedagogy.

As you might suspect, *Can It Really Be Taught?: Resisting Lore in Creative Writing Pedagogy*, a collection edited by Kelly Ritter and myself which came out in 2007, sought specifically to lay the title question (an old cocktail party saw, at least among literary types) to rest or at least advance the conversation about the teaching of creative writing beyond the Romantic myths that surround it. These include myths about rigor, grading, even about writers and writing in popular culture itself. That same year, moreover, Edinburgh University Press/Columbia University Press brought out *The Handbook of Creative*

Writing. Edited by Steve Earnshaw of Sheffield Hallam University in the UK, and targeting teachers and students alike, the massive *Handbook* features forty-eight chapters in three parts: i) critical theories behind practice; ii) "how to" basics on the central genres and iii) advice on the practicalities of the writing life.

Most recently, noted UK poet and playwright Michelene Wandor has provided the first book-length history of creative writing in Britain, *The Author is Not Dead, Merely Somewhere Else*, a book that advances several critical conversations about the methodology of the workshop and Creative Writing's position in higher education in the English-speaking world. Meanwhile, Graeme Harper and Australian author Jeri Kroll have added *Creative Writing Studies: Practice, Research and Pedagogy*, a collection of thirteen essays, with an afterword from D.W. Fenza (drawn from his *Chronicle* essays), that probe all three areas of the subtitle in order to examine "the integrated nature" of creative writing in higher education.

In fact, Harper and Kroll's *Creative Writing Studies* may be viewed as a fitting antecedent to Tim Mayer's article in the January 2009 issue of *College English* "One Simple Word: From Creative Writing to Creative Writing Studies." This special issue on Creative Writing in the twenty-first century was also assembled with an eye towards moving the field forward in innovative ways, suggesting new paths and provoking new debates and discussions.

This brings us to March 2009 and the composition of this chapter. It bears repeating: this is hardly an exhaustive bibliography. Surely I have left out many fine, perhaps more genre-specific, volumes and a long list of articles. Anyone seeking a more comprehensive grouping of sources might begin by cobbling together the bibliographic appendices from Bishop's *Released into Language*, and the indices available from *New Writing*, as well as the bibliographic appendices in *Teaching Creative Writing to Undergraduates: A Resource and Guide*, that Kelly Ritter and I have written for the Fountainhead Press Professional Development X Series.

As Stephen Healey's 2009 assessment of Creative Writing as a discipline began, *in media res*, so ends this chapter, in the midst of what I hope will be an ongoing story, the story of creative writers in higher education reflecting on and attending to the theory and pedagogy of their field with a fuller understanding of the rich history, the work, the lives and the stories, that preceded them. It is, in a sense, a modest effort at giving Wendy Bishop what she asked for, in return for the many gifts her life and legacy gave us. It is a place to start.

Chapter Five

Creative Writing Programs in the World

Although I have long felt that writing programs in higher education miss a momentous opportunity if they fail to make deep and lasting connections to the wider community, the timing for such initiatives, as I write this, in mid 2010, could not be more critical. Still reeling from the global economic crisis of 2008–09, which saw massive layoffs at publishing houses, frozen and discontinued lists and abandoned authors, the publishing industry is grappling with the rise of the e-book and all the attendant anxiety surrounding a technology that will undoubtedly change the way people read, indeed, the way people interact with written word. Concurrent with this cultural shift, new media – including but not limited to such wide ranging developments as social media, interactive gaming, and publishing on demand – are altering the way writing is created and narrative is processed. No wonder vigorous debates on the future of publishing rage on.

Recognizing flux: Engaging in new ways
Not all predictions have been dire – some have been quite positive – but the atmosphere of instability has taken its toll. Global responses to this instability, however, vary. Some industry insiders – whether editor, publisher or author (often teaching in a university or college writing program) – decry the lack of gatekeeping in the digital realm, bemoaning the fact that anyone can write any kind of "drivel" and publish it digitally to mass audiences that

grow larger by the minute. Others engage with this growing audience and the present state of flux directly – to wit the Australia Council for the Arts' embrace of digital media in such projects as *Story of the Future* (and the companion guide it engendered, *The Writer's Guide to Making a Digital Living: Choose Your Own Adventure* (Australia Council for the Arts 2008). Created in partnership with the Australian Film Television and Radio School, *Story of the Future* is a project designed to help "writers develop digital interactive and cross platform narratives for the twenty-first century." It achieves these ends via "seminars in digital writing and digital publishing with leading international experts [and] project development residential labs" as well as through grant-making and strengthening industry and research/creativity connections. *The Writer's Guide to Making A Digital Living*, moreover, available both in an *interactive* online format and in the more traditional PDF form, anticipates the inevitable displacement conventionally-trained creative writers might face in this new digital economy and shows them, as well as more digitally savvy authors, how to find a place in it. Although developed primarily in Australia, these initiatives have an international reach and should be required reading for arts administrators, creative writing educators and writers themselves worldwide as one model for the ways in which artists, educators and arts agencies can engage with these new audiences and formats.

Conversely, in the United States in 2007, the National Endowment for the Arts published "To Read or Not to Read: A Question of National Consequence," a document that summarized a number of studies of reading among cross-sections of the American public and declared reading at serious risk. Among American teenagers and young adults, the report cited "a historical decline in voluntary reading rates … a gradual worsening of reading skills among older teens [and] declining proficiency in adult readers" (2007, p. 19). Widely criticized for its narrow definition of "reading," "voluntary reading," and "literature," (the report does not include creative nonfiction in its definition of literature, for example, eliminating a highly popular form of reading in the past decade), as well as for applying "traditional" solutions ,(e.g. community reading programs like the "Big Read") to an increasingly nontraditional audience, "To Read or Not to Read" nonetheless makes several important points. Chief among these is the fact that lower levels of reading and writing ability severely handicap citizens in the job market, leading to "lack of employment, lower wages, and fewer opportunities for advancement" (Gioia 2007, p. 3). Even in the UK, which boasts one of the highest literacy rates in the world, among employers, "concerns over staff literacy are widespread. Of employers who rate the competency of their low-skilled staff as poor, half report problems with literacy" (National Literacy Trust 2010, p. 5). Literacy-challenged populations are also "less likely to become active in civic and *cultural* life" (emphasis mine) (Gioia 2007, p. 4). Prominent among these reports, moreover, is the fact that low literacy rates impact the most socioeconomically fragile in our society, those least likely to be reared in print-rich homes and attend high-performing schools. Those of us holding this book in our hands know that reading and writing "powerfully" (Gioia) changes lives, and yet that power is denied to those in our society most in need of it. What are we to make of such profound injustice? What should we do about it?

It is easy, in the face of such overwhelming inequity, to lay the blame elsewhere, at the feet of primary and secondary education perhaps, on the doorsteps of libraries or in the realm of popular culture, to shake our heads disapprovingly and carry on, writing books for increasingly smaller audiences, leading creative writing workshops populated, for the most part, by the more privileged members of our society – in short, talking only to each other. Regardless of where the problem originated, however, it is well within the hands of artists and writers, especially those in higher education, to become part of the solution. I believe it is incumbent upon us to do so. Moreover, creative writing programs in higher education not only have a responsibility to connect with local, regional and global communities in ways that overcome inequity and build a sense of civic duty in their students, they also have a vested interest in such initiatives, in community partnerships that expand and enlarge literate culture. What's more, they're better positioned – with the resources, infrastructure, and human (student) power – than most institutions, to do so.

At this point in the volume, you may be picturing your writing time vanishing into the ether, considering such initiatives just one more distraction better left to political and social activists, not writers. Enter the three programs of note I am about to describe, inspiring programs conceived and implemented, in fact, by writers. Successful, prolific writers with a social conscience. These programs demonstrate that the kind of social responsibility my colleague, Ball State University professor and fiction writer Cathy Day describes as "literary citizenship," can survive and thrive, to both contribute to the communities in which they operate and to the lives of the writers who serve in them while, importantly, enhancing readership at large.

826 National: A serendipitous confluence
The brainchild of acclaimed novelist Dave Eggers (*A Heartbreaking Work of Staggering Genius, What is the What, You Shall Know Our Velocity* and *Zeitun*, among others) and public teacher Ninive Clements Calegari, 826 was founded in 2002 as 826 Valencia, named for its street location in the Mission District of San Francisco, with the aim of providing a "writing and publishing center that would promote literacy and book devouring" (Eggers 2008, p. 2) and form a "bridge between teachers, students and the community" (826 National Video 2010). In Calegari's words,

> Dave was realizing that for him and his friends who were doing freelance work, there were ebbs and flows in the work that came their way. So here was a group of highly skilled people that could be tapped, in a flexible way, to do something good for society. Dave wanted to pay special attention to people working in publishing, the industry he knew best, and he wanted to work with students. It was a serendipitous confluence of people and events.
>
> (Kelley 2008)

Many of Eggers' friends were teachers or former teachers, and he was familiar with the San Francisco public schools from the time when he raised his younger brother there, upon the practically simultaneous deaths of their parents from cancer (famously chronicled in *A Staggering Work*); experiences that gave him an insider's view of not only "the hazards of falling behind in language skills" (Eggers qtd. in Ganahl 2002) in our society but also the monumental task teachers face in reaching individual writers in classrooms overcrowded with students. "When we learned more about it," Eggers says, "we realized that with a little one-on-one tutoring, we could help kids improve by leaps and bounds fairly quickly" (qtd. in Ganahl 2002).

With that realization came action; Eggers and Calegari found office space on the now legendary 826 Valencia Street, gathered together their willing writing and publishing friends, hung out a shingle (actually a sandwich board) reading "free tutoring," and waited for their first clients.

They didn't have to wait long. In fact, the initiative took off with astonishing speed. Writers, artists and publishing industry professionals "rushed to help with the project, either by volunteering to tutor, teach workshops or by sending a page of a manuscript to be framed and hung on the back wall" (Ganahl). By late 2005, the concept had spread to five other cities, with 826 chapters opening in New York City, Los Angeles, Chicago, Seattle and Michigan. The framework is fairly simple, with volunteers setting up shop and "offering tutoring sessions to kids in the neighborhood" (Saracevic 2008, p. 3). During the day, the volunteers might work on their own publishing projects, including Eggers' literary journal *McSweeney's*. But "when school lets out, the kids come in to do their homework and work on projects with one-on-one help. In many cases, the kids work up anthologies [of their writing] that get published" (Saracevic).

The secrets of 826 National's success are many, but perhaps most notable are a youthful atmosphere and direct contact with practicing writers. The first came about almost by accident. When Eggers and Calegari set out to rent 826 Valencia, they were told the space was only zoned for retail. They solved this problem by adding a storefront to the center, a pirate supply shop that enhances the kid-friendly atmosphere and also contributes to the non-profit's coffers. The venture was so successful, in fact, as a fund-raiser and ice-breaker, that the rest of the six chapters were founded with their own storefronts. As a result, kids are tutored at 826 NYC under the auspices of the Brooklyn Superhero Supply Co., in Los Angeles at the Echo Park Time Travel Mart, in Chicago at The Boring Store, in Seattle at the Greenwood Space Travel Supply Company and in Ann Arbor, Michigan at the Liberty Street Robot Supply and Repair Store. Founders of the Boston chapter, the youngest of the seven, gave the storefront idea a twist, however, with the Greater Boston Bigfoot Research Center.

The fact that tutors in the center are practicing writers adds to the students' experience, a theme that is also key to the success of the other two programs I will describe later. When asked how tutors engage the most reluctant readers and writers, Ninive Calegari points out that "the people who teach at our centers are real cartoonists and real journalists ... the kids are part of an apprenticeship experience with a dude who actually does the same job in the real world" (Kelley 2008, p.2). Notes "real" writer George Saunders, "in a time when everyone is bemoaning the decline in literacy ... 826 is an incredibly innovative, energetic way to say to kids that language is power" (qtd. in Freymann-Weyr 2008, p. 1). Since 2002, tens of thousands of students have gotten this message. In 2005, *Time* magazine named Dave Eggers one of its 100 most influential people, citing his influence as stemming "less from his original voice than from parlaying his success into a combination of indie publishing empire, literary circle and social works project" (Poniwozik 2005). Thanks to the dedication of Eggers and his colleagues across the country the 826 centers have become a national treasure.

The Arvon Foundation: Because writing matters

The legendary Arvon Foundation in the United Kingdom began in 1968 under modest but perhaps uniquely British conditions, emerging after a long series of pub conversations between writers John Fairfax and John Moat about "creating a salient into the school system by enabling young people eager to write to spend a few days living as and working with experienced writers" (Moat 2005, p. 25). Soon enough, the two authors put their words into action by commandeering a retreat space from a rural arts center in South West England to provide a residential writers workshop for a group of secondary students from a local school. Meeting that first night, they told these students all they knew about them was that they were interested in writing. In John Moat's words, "we told them that we had that in common and that the next days would be theirs, their own writing time. We said we were poets and that the only thing special about poets was their belief that poems were important and that time spent working on poems wasn't a waste of time" (2005 p. 29). John Fairfax, in fact, had been born into an artistic family but knew that his situation was highly unusual and that more common was "the isolation experienced by many ... young writers ... for whom there was no readily available affirmation or guidance from practising artists" (Moat 2005, p. 13). The two writers were also friends with future poet laureate Ted Hughes, who they invited to come listen to the young people read on the final night of the retreat. Of that evening, Moat writes: "Maybe the poems weren't more exceptional than every poem needs to be. But, as I remember it, there was a thread to them, and each one a discovery that enlarged on the discovery of those four days. Light from the poems seemed to filter into the room – the gleam of being young, having been out in the sun and handed the moon and given the key" (p. 33).

There was little disagreement that the experience was a success. Later the headmaster of the school pronounced that students who'd attended that first retreat had experienced a profound change in attitude that had "a beneficial effect on the performance of their entire year" (p. 46). Perhaps sensing the enormity of what they were about to begin, Moat and Fairfax were reluctant at first to develop the potential of their endeavor, but eventually "accepted that if something useful *had* come out of our experiment, we weren't entirely free to do nothing about it" (p. 37).

Ted Hughes was also affected by that first Arvon experience, becoming one of the Foundation's strongest supporters, and certainly, his prominence had an influence on drawing resources and other writers to the project. According to John Moat, "there were few Arvon meetings he'd not be involved with, little committees, ad hoc brainstorming sessions ... high and low level delegations" (p. 26). Hughes also donated Lumb Bank, in West

113

Yorkshire, making Arvon in the north possible. And later, "when Arvon's debt seemed bound to bring it down," Hughes "dreamed up and then engineer[ed] the first Arvon International Poetry Competition in 1980" which drew over 30,000 paid entries and exhausted its judges: Hughes, Seamus Heaney, Charles Causley and Philip Larkin. The competition saved the Foundation, however, and not incidentally, named another future Poet Laureate, Andrew Motion, as the winner (p. 26).

Although its primary aim was to serve young, fledgling student-writers, Arvon soon expanded to include teachers and later, the general population; anyone who was interested in exploring their world via writing. By reaching out to teachers, the Foundation was the "first initiative … that recognized the centrality of teachers' creativity to their role in education" (p. 52). In fact, Moat suggests that some writers in the schools programs fail by not involving the *teachers* in writing, and in doing so, "they undermine teacher's self-belief with the inference that 'doing creativity' is something they're not up to," (p. 52). This recognition is also the foundation of the National Writing Project in the US (www.nwp.org), begun by educator James Graves at approximately the same time and aimed directly at cultivating the teacher as writer. The success of both organizations hinges on the understanding that teachers who believe the myth that creativity is gifted sparingly among the population are likely to perpetuate that myth among their students. Likewise, teachers who understand that writing and creativity belong to them as much as anyone else will empower their students to exercise their right to write and to grow as writers.

In 2006, during my study tour of the UK, Manchester Metropolitan University creative writing faculty member Heather Beck generously invited me along on an Arvon workshop she was leading at Lumb Bank. The experience was profound and, as I understand from John Moat's memoir, typically Arvon. I was given a tiny, austere attic room with a bed, desk and chair, one that, despite my scholarly protestations against the perpetuation of the "mythological" garret, was probably the closest to such a place I will ever experience and as such wore down my resistance. Later, before a dinner that was communally prepared and served and would be for the remainder of the week (another hallmark of the Arvon experience), we were given a genial list of the "rules" that would enhance our experience (one of which was, if we were to venture into town, to refrain, at all costs and in all seriousness, from "beating the locals in the trivia game at the pub," so as not to undermine a relationship with the community that had been painstakingly cultivated over the years). I was given plenty of time to write, in my attic room and in the many idyllic red sheds strategically placed throughout the property, outfitted with just enough room for my person, a chair and a writing surface built into the wall. Above this, the lone window framed a spectacular few of the mist rising from the Pennine hills. I filled many pages in my notebook that day, observing at one point that the only thing missing from my experience in this writer's hut was a gentle rain, which immediately commenced. Later, I was invited to join the workshop participants in a writing exercise led by Paul Magrs and my work shared, accepted and critiqued along with everyone else's, despite my status as a stranger and "observer" to boot.

If this rendition of my experience sounds overly rosy, and perhaps too enamored of the lore-suffused writing experience I had out in the British countryside, I make no apologies. Because what is – and was – essential about that Arvon experience is that the experience is available to *anyone* who wants to take it, who wants to try a few days away from the spinning world exploring their writing among kindred spirits. The many, rather than the few, are validated as writers.

Since 1968, the Arvon Foundation has grown to include four Writing Houses that provide residential writing retreats year round and to employ hundreds of renowned writers to lead them – a list that reads as a virtual who's who of the British literary world. Hewing closely to the founding desire to give participants belief in the power of their own words, the Foundation is process- rather than result-driven, as Moat underscores when he writes, "whether the outcome of all this for the student [is] the distinctiveness of a secret journal or a best-seller...they were equally not the concern of Arvon ... except in as much as they were what the student wanted to write" (p. 48). In the same vein, Arvon is also "militantly non-exclusive...always open to anyone interested in exploring their gift to write" (p. 46). Indeed, Moat takes great pride in the fact that on the beginners course at Lumb Bank, supper might include "a world war II survivor ... and the Countess of Stowe already and irretrievably in conversation with the Secretary of the Nottingham Miners Union" (p. 88).

In his evaluation of the very first Arvon workshop, under Moat and Fairfax's tutelage, one student wrote, "We had been called to write as if writing mattered ... I think what was shattering was that suddenly, everything mattered" (p. 99). Such a succinct embodiment of the Arvon philosophy, the philosophy of a foundation founded by writers and developed, over the decades, by writers, into one of the most influential organizations in the world of creative writing. Because writing matters, everything matters.

The Virginia G. Piper Center for Creative Writing: Bringing the University and the Community Together

So far, our model programs have been founded, implemented and developed by writers; proof positive that we can act in powerful ways to impact the literacy of the community at large, to combat educational inequity and social injustice in ways that do not threaten our literary careers but may, in fact, expand our audience. The crux of my argument, however, is that creative writing programs in higher education are even better positioned to influence the promotion of literary culture as a result of existing infrastructures and resources both human and to a lesser extent, financial, and that it is, in fact, to the benefit of their students and the general population that they take this position seriously. The Virginia G. Piper Center for Creative Writing at Arizona State University embodies this argument, asserting that it aims to provide the "southwest hub for writers and readers and the artistic and intellectual hub of a newly vibrant, multinational and culturally diverse world of writers...as well as the driving force for a dynamic and entrepreneurial creative environment that will enrich Arizona and global communities" (2010 http://www.asu.edu/piper/).

The heart of this Center is undoubtedly the Piper Writers House, located in the former President's Cottage on Arizona State University's campus. This historic property was renovated in 2005 to provide optimal space that "'brings the university community and the greater Phoenix community together as a home for creative writing,' explains Elizabyth Hiscox, the Piper House program coordinator" (Weaver 2009). Included in this space, which is also open to the public, is not only room for classes and seminars, but also administrative offices, a library, and an archive for Arizona State University literary history, while the grounds outside include performance areas and a writers garden (http://www.asu.edu/piper/about/writershouse/writershouse.html). The library, moreover, is a specialized resource center that not only "provides resources for creative writers in the [MFA] program but also in the community at large," (Weaver 2009) subscribing to over forty literary journals and writing publications.

Although the Piper Center is a non-academic unit, it is considered a complement to the academic Creative Writing MFA program at ASU that was founded in 1984 and provides numerous opportunities for students in that program to become involved in local and global outreach. Local programs, for example, include the Young Writers at Work Classroom, which sends graduate students to teach for "one to two week residencies...in settings where participants are not likely themselves to become writers" (http://english.clas.asu.edu/cw-reachoutprograms), an initiative which began with a partnership with the Phoenix Public Library in 1985. In 1999, the Center expanded its reach to youth by joining with the Arizona Office of Youth Programs to provide elementary and secondary school students "with creative writing programs designed to foster an understanding and enthusiasm for writing as a lifelong skill, providing classroom teachers with ideas for curriculum enhancement and providing opportunities for MFA students to develop as teaching artists" (http:// english.clas.asu.edu/cw-reachoutprograms).

Arizona outreach has since grown exponentially to include reservations, hospitals, detention centers, and Alzheimer's units (http://www.asu.edu/piper/az_outreach/index.html). At the 2009 AWP Conference, I listened to one of these students describe how she wandered the halls of the Mayo Clinic, stopping by the rooms of receptive- looking patients to ask "if I can come in and visit with them and we can write a poem together" (http://wordamour.wordpress.com/2009/02/14/live-from-chicago-awp-2009-day-2/), an exercise in what the woman called "lyric medicine." Not surprisingly, in such a socially active program, outreach does not stop in Arizona. A global outreach initiative provides fellowships that have allowed graduate students to teach in, among other countries, China, Singapore, the United Kingdom and the Czech Republic (http://www.asu.edu/clas/pipercwcenter/global_outreach/fellowships/index.html).

It is no coincidence that this chapter ends with the richly varied university-community partnership at Arizona State University, a testament to the fact that not only are such programs possible but that they bring numerous benefits to the community *and* to the students who have the opportunity to develop their skills as writers with a social conscience. While the Virginia G. Piper Center is not the only community-university partnership among graduate programs in creative writing, it is clear that service and outreach may very well be the lifeblood of the program at

119

Arizona State University, from its earliest days.

Obviously, the Piper Center is very well funded by the Virginia G. Piper Charitable Trust, but just as obvious is the fact that such initiatives *attract* funding, for they demonstrate an institution's dedication to looking beyond its borders, to transforming the graduate program from a mere cash cow to one with a long-term commitment not only to its own students but also the immediate community and the world beyond. The same could be said for 826 National and the Arvon Foundation, institutions who attract the attention, involvement and monetary support of writers and literary patrons (literary luminaries and entertainers such as Michael Chabon and Jon Stewart in the US, Mark Haddon and Waterstone's Books in the UK), proof that underwriting for the kinds of programs that promote the relationship between literary citizenship *and* literate culture is available for those who seek it. A growing number of graduate programs in creative writing have begun to realize the importance of reaching out to the community. Imagine the world that would result if all of them did. A world of writers *and* readers.

Afterword

Looking Inward and Outward

Once, years ago, during a conversation about writing, Richard Bausch quoted Jesus from the Gospel of Thomas: "If you bring forth what is within you, what you have will save you." Bausch then revised the rest of the phrase to add that if you do not bring forth what is within you, it will destroy you. Writers, we are told, write because they have something to say, that they simply must say. In *Writing a Book that Makes a Difference*, Philip Gerard tells us, "Every writer has a book he *needs* to write" (2000, p. 2).

This book is not fiction, poetry, drama or creative nonfiction (although it includes some memoir). But it is the book I needed to write.

Once, years ago, someone told me that "creative writing theory pedagogy" is what people write before they get tenure, after which they turn to the "real work" of imaginative writing itself, the work we would all rather be doing than anything else.

I have been a tenured associate professor for several years. In that time I have continued to write about the teaching of creative writing: two more books (counting this one) and many essays and articles. During those years I have also continued to write and publish creative nonfiction, have written a novel that is waiting patiently to be revised, and have a book-length memoir and another novel in the planning stages. These projects are vitally important to me and I look forward to returning to them.

But this was the book I needed to write.

When my work on creative writing pedagogy encounters resistance, it is often based on the assumption that some of the flaws and problems I see in the system are based on experiences I had over twenty years ago (despite my complete immersion in the field since then). "Things have changed," the protests go. "It's not like that anymore."

At the same time, writing in parallel to this work are those who ask, repeatedly and almost innocently, in major venues (*The Writer's Chronicle*, *Poets and Writers*, *College Composition and Communication*) and at major conferences as if for the *very first time*: Can creative writing be taught? What am I doing when I teach it? If I wanted to teach it better, where would I even look? There seems to be some lore or myths associated with creative writing – am I the only one who's noticed?

From where I stand, mouth agape: two completely different responses that cancel each other out.

This was the book I needed to write and in writing it, my central goals are these:

1. To make the discipline that is creative writing theory and pedagogy far more visible; to say, in effect, we are here, there are legions of us, without and within creative writing programs, and we want to talk about making them better – after all, isn't the human tendency, we like to think, toward improvement? We want to expand the conversation but we want those who join us there to have some sense of what has been said before, to lurk a little while before jumping in. It's only polite, after all.

2. Once this conversation expands, to initiate and encourage a culture of reflection in creative writing classrooms and programs, to implore writers, teachers, program directors to continually ask, what are we doing

well? What could we be doing better? Whose voices are we listening to? Whose voices are not being heard? As professors (and underclasses of adjuncts), are we merely reproducing ourselves, in class, gender, race or are we widening our reach, looking for ways to make a life with words possible for those who don't look like us, who haven't had our advantages? These are just *some* of the questions that might be asked; what is important is that we ask them.

3. More personal but directly dependent on the first two: that the next generation of novice writers will learn and develop in an environment where the curriculum is not a foregone conclusion, a dead icon, its edges resistant and brittle, but a living, breathing evolving space.

I am hopeful. For one thing, I have tried, in this book, to offer a blueprint for how work toward these goals might proceed, both for those new to the discipline and casting about for guidance and for those veterans who are ready for a change. For another, I have to begun to see flickers of this change. Pedagogy sessions continue to grow in number, and, albeit slowly, in topic diversity at the AWP Conference in the US every year, while the UK and Australasia each continue to develop their own individual, considered, creative writing disciplines, along their own trajectories, rich with publications and resources. All three of us are poised, if we can continue what has so far been a nascent inter-Anglophile exchange, to take advantage of a flattening world and learn what each has to offer the other. And then there is the international community, postsecondary creative writing programs emergent in Sweden, India, Greece, just to name a few. What will they bring to our creative writing institutions? What will we bring to theirs? Perhaps globalization will force the traditionalists' hands, reawaken those who are mid-Western idealists in the spirit of Paul Engle who originally sought to bring the world to Iowa in the name of innovation.

None of this potential can be realized, however, if we respond to these changes with knee-jerk resistance, clinging to the status quo. We must be ready to constantly examine our curricula, classrooms, practices, welcoming the efforts of those who lead us in these directions.

I am also a long time associate of the National Writing Project (NWP), a director of one of more than 200 sites across the nation in this university-elementary-and secondary school partnership to improve the teaching of writing in the US. A nearly forty-year-old organization, we are also regarded as one of the premier models of educational reform in the country. It would be easy for such a program to rest on these kinds of laurels, to keep on doing what it's always been doing because, after all, it seems to work.

Recently, however, at a national program leaders meeting, the NWP brought in a keynote speaker, a writer-scholar, to share the research she had been doing on the organization and the sites and practices within it, to try and puzzle out what was effective and why, and what was not.

A keynote speaker. Telling us what we were doing right and what we might, as a group and as individuals within it, consider looking at more closely, more reflectively in order to improve our service to our teachers and students.

I tried to imagine a creative writing researcher invited to keynote a creative writing conference in the US or featured prominently in the pages of a major publication in the field. It was difficult. Less than six months later, when a writer who had been studying MFA programs and writing about them *for years* made his work public in a *Poets and Writers* article examining and ranking them, the wrath of AWP was fierce and immediate. I no longer had to imagine.

The creative writing frontier, at least in the Anglophile realm, is closed. We no longer need to circle the wagons to protect creative writing in higher education as we clear a path in the wilderness. The luxury of turning our gaze to our students, the essential core of this endeavor, is ours if we choose it and the future looks good, so long as we recognize that everything we need to know to move toward an institutional culture of reflection is either before us or within us. We need only teach ourselves to look and to bring forth what we see. And as writers, upon whom, as Henry James famously wrote, "nothing is lost," such a culture seems well within our grasp.

Appendix

Honor Roll of Graduate Creative Writing Programs

These programs, some well known and some obscure, are listed because they provide a considered, expanded curriculum of experiences for students, like those in the detailed list of programs in chapter three, that enhance their graduate experience in *at least* one area: teaching, publishing, community service, creative industry connections. They are not ranked, but listed in alphabetical order.*

Bath Spa University	Bath, UK
Indiana University	Bloomington, IN
Middlesex University	London, UK
Minnesota State University	Mankato, MN
New York University	New York, NY
Rosemont College	Philadelphia, PA
Sarah Lawrence College	Bronxville, NY
University of Arizona	Tucson, AZ
University of Winchester	Winchester, UK
Virginia Polytechnic Institute	Blacksburg, VA

*Programs outside North America and the UK are not listed, solely because the author's knowledge of their individual curricula is at this writing not of sufficient depth to accurately isolate any for commendation.

Acknowledgements

This book has been several years in the making and as such, it owes a debt to many people and institutions. I am deeply grateful to the University of Central Arkansas, particularly to the Faculty Research Fund, for the sabbatical and the financial support that made my study tour possible, and to Elaine MacNiece, Vice Provost and Dean of the Graduate School, Rollin Potter, Dean of the College of Fine Arts and Communication, Scott Payne, Chair of the Department of Creative Writing, and especially to my former chair, David R. Harvey. It bears repeating that his continued support of my research into creative writing pedagogy, a most unconventional field in the early years of my career, was instrumental in giving me the academic freedom to pursue my passion.

In addition, I owe a great debt to the community of international creative writing scholars who paved the way before me and journey alongside me in this discipline: to Graeme Harper for answering my first tentative email all those many years ago, to Kelly Ritter, for her years of friendship and wise collaboration, to the late Wendy Bishop, for her generosity and trailblazing, to Anthony and Karen Haynes, for having the vision to found *The Professional and Higher Partnership* with a special focus on the field of creative writing, and to the following writers and scholars for making my professional life all the richer: Patrick Bizzaro, Kendall Dunkelberg, Anna Leahy, Cathy Day, Mary Cantrell, Tim Mayers, Katharine Haake, Mary Ann Cain, Mimi Thebo, Philip Gross, Steve May,

Michelene Wandor, Richard Kerridge and Paul Munden. Philip Gerard's interview provided a critical window to the founding of a twenty-first century creative writing program and I am grateful for the time he took to answer my questions. I am also grateful for Karen Haynes' meticulous editing; it is no small thing to be reminded with every query that your work is in such good hands.

Also empowering has been my work with the National Writing Project and the professional community I found there, with Elyse Eidman-Aadahl, Lynette Herring-Harris, Ann Dobie, and especially Monda Fason and Mike Rush. Writers and friends Erika Dreifus, William Lychack, Chris Motto, Dawn Stahlberg and Hannah Treitel Cosdon have also long made my real and virtual worlds a better place.

I am grateful for the publishers' permission to reprint the following material: "Once More to the Workshop: A Myth Caught in Time," which first appeared in *Does the Writing Workshop Still Work?* Dianne Donnelly ed. 2010, Multilingual Matters; "Storming the Garret," originally published in *Writing in Education* (43) 2007, National Association of Writers in Education; and "Grasping Ariadne's Thread: Wendy Bishop's Stories and My Own," in *Composing Ourselves as Writer-Teacher-Writers*, Patrick Bizzaro, Devan Cook and Alys Culhane eds, forthcoming from Hampton Press.

Finally, this book would not exist without the support of my family: my extended family, a generous and genial lot, and my immediate family, my two sons, Jackson and Will, and especially my husband, John, whose constant demonstration of love as a verb makes all things possible.

References

Abramson, Seth 2009. "The Top 50 MFA Programs in the US: A Comprehensive Guide," *Poets & Writers* November/December 88–91

Adams, Katharine 1993. *A History of Professional Writing Instruction in American Colleges: Years of Acceptance, Growth and Doubt.* Dallas, SMUP

Australasian Association of Writing Programs 2010. "Writing Courses," http://www.aawp.org.au/courses, accessed April 30 2010

Australia Council for the Arts 2008. "Story of the Future," http://www.australiacouncil.gov.au/the_arts/projects/about_story_of_the_future, accessed May 28 2010

—"The Writer's Guide to Making a Digital Living," http://www.australiacouncil.gov.au/writersguide, accessed May 28 2010

Barden, Dan 2008. "Workshop: A Rant Against Creative Writing Classes," *Poets & Writers* http://www.pw.org/content/workshop_rant_against_creative_writing_classes, accessed May 31 2010

Bausch, Richard 2010. "How to Write in 700 Easy Lessons: The Case Against Writing Manuals," *The Atlantic Fiction Supplement 2010*, 28–31

Becker, Geoff 2010. "Program Directors Talk Shop." AWP Conference, Denver April 9

Bishop, Wendy, Katharine Haake, Hans Ostrum (eds.) 1994. *Colors of a Different Horse: Rethinking Creative Writing Theory and Pedagogy.* Carbondale, National Council of Teachers of English

Bishop, Wendy 2005. "Contracts, Radical Revision, Portfolios and the Risks of Writing," in *Power and Identity in the Creative Writing Classroom: The Authority Project,* Anna Leahy ed. Clevedon, Multilingual Matters

—1998. *Released Into Language.* Carbondale, National Council of Teachers of English

—1997. *Teaching Lives: Essays and Stories.* Logan, Utah State University Press

Bizzaro, Patrick 1993. *Responding to Student Poems: Applications of Critical Theory.* Carbondale, National Council of Teachers of English

Brook, Scott 2009. "Accounting for Creative Writing: Preliminary Report of the Accounting for Creative Writing Student Survey," http://aawp.org.au/files/Preliminaryreportof the accountingforcreativewritingsurvey.pdf, accessed April 26 2010

Brophy, Kevin 2008. "Workshopping the Workshop and Teaching the Unteachable," in *Creative Writing Studies,* Harper, Graeme and Jeri Kroll, eds. Clevedon, Multilingual Matters

Butt, Maggie, Steve May, Robyn Bolam and Helena Blakemore 2008. "Writers in the World." http://www.nawe.co.uk/DB/wie-editions/articles/writers-in-the-world.html, accessed June 1 2010

Cain, Mary Ann 1995. *Revisioning Writers' Talk: Gender and Culture in Acts of Composing.* Albany, State University of New York Press

Chasar, Mike 2008. "Remembering Paul Engle," *The Writer's Chronicle* November/December

Coles, Robert 1990. *The Call of Stories: Teaching and the Moral Imagination.* Boston, Houghton Mifflin

Connor, Peter 2005. "Ariadne," *Gods, Goddesses, and Mythology*, Vol. 2. New York, Marshall Cavendish

Dawson, Paul 2005. *Creative Writing and the New Humanities*. London, Routledge

Delaney, Edward J. 2007. "Where Great Writers Are Made: Assessing America's Top Graduate Writing Programs," *The Atlantic Fiction Supplement* http://www.theatlantic. com/magazine/archive/2007/08/where-great-writers-are-made/6032/, accessed March 14 2010

De la Torre, Miguel 2007. *Liberating Jonah: Forming an Ethics of Reconciliation*. Phoenix, Orbis

Donnelly, Dianne 2010. "Introduction: If it Ain't Broke, Don't Fix it; Or Change Is Inevitable, Except From a Vending Machine," in *Does the Writing Workshop Still Work?* Dianne Donnelly, ed. Clevedon, Multilingual Matters 1–29

Earnshaw, Steven, ed. 2007. *The Handbook of Creative Writing*. Edinburgh UP

Editorial Anonymous 2010. "Sexy, Sexy Armadillos," http://editorialanonymous.blogspot.com/2010/04/sexy-sexy-armadillos.html, accessed April 28, 2010

Eggers, Dave 2008. "The Future of Words," http://www.esquire.com/features/75-most-influential/dave-eggers-1008, accessed May 29, 2010

Fenza, David 2009. "A Brief History of AWP," http://www.awpwriter.org/aboutawp/index.htm, accessed April 2 2010

—2001. "Creative Writing and Its Discontents," http://www.awpwriter.org/magazine/writers/fenza01.htm, accessed March 14 2010

Fleisher, Kass 2002. "Scenes from the Battlefield: A Feminist Resists the Writing Workshop," *The Iowa*

Review 22: 1, 109–115.

Florida, Richard 2002. *The Rise of the Creative Class: And How It's Transforming Work, Leisure, Community and Everyday Life.* New York, Basic Books

Freymann-Weyr, Jeffrey 2008. "Fighting for Truth, Justice and Creativity," http://www.npr.org/templates/story/story.php?storyId=90776483, accessed May 26 2010

Ganahl, Jane 2002. "A Heartbreaking Work of Literary Altruism," http://articles.sfgate.com/2002-08-02/news/17556162_1_pirate-supply-store-writing-workshops, accessed May 26 2010

Gerard, Philip 2000. *Writing a Book that Makes a Difference.* Cincinnati, Story Press

— 2010. Email to author. June 1 2010

Gioia, Dana 2007. "Preface: Executive Summary," *To Read or Not to Read: A Question of National Consequence.* http://www.nea.gov/research/ToRead_ExecSum.pdf, accessed May 26, 2010

Grimes, Tom 1999. *The Workshop: Seven Decades of the Iowa Workshop – 43 Stories, Recollections and Essays on Iowa's Place in 20th Century American Literature.* New York, Hyperion

Gross, Philip 2010. "Small Worlds: What Works in Workshops If and When They Do?" in *Does the Writing Workshop Still Work?* Dianne Donnelly, ed. Clevedon, Multilingual Matters, 52–62

Haake, Katharine 2000. *What Our Speech Disrupts: Feminism and Creative Writing Studies.* Carbondale, National Council of Teachers of English

Harper, Graeme and Jeri Kroll, eds. 2008. *Creative Writing Studies: Practice, Research & Pedagogy.* Clevedon, Multilingual Matters

Harper, Graeme, ed. 2006. *Teaching Creative Writing.* London, Continuum

Healey, Steve 2009. "The Rise of Creative Writing and the New Value of Creativity," *The Writer's Chronicle,* January/February

Houghton, Timothy 2006. "Letters," *Profession: A Publication of the Modern Language Association,* 198

Kealey, Tom 2008. *The Creative Writing MFA Handbook.* London, Continuum

Kelley, Lauren 2008. "Five Questions for Ninive Clements Calegari," *Philanthropy News Digest,* http://foundationcenter.org/pnd, accessed May 26 2010

Kupfer, Fern 2003. "The Dream, and the Reality, of Writing Fiction," *Chronicle of Higher Education: Chronicle Review* 49:20, B5

Lamott, Anne 1995. *Bird by Bird: Some Instructions on Writing and Life.* New York, Anchor

Leahy, Anna 2005, ed. *Power and Identity in the Creative Writing Classroom: The Authority Project.* Clevedon, Multilingual Matters

— 2010. "Teaching as a Creative Act: Why the Workshop Works in Creative Writing," in *Does the Writing Workshop Still Work?* Dianne Donnelly, ed. Clevedon, Multilingual Matters, 63–77

Light, Greg 2002. "How Students Understand and Learn Creative Writing in Higher Education," *Writing in Education,* http://www.nawe.co.uk/DB/wie-editions/articles/how-students-understand-and-learn-creative-writing.html, accessed June 2 2010

Lloyd, Carol 1997. *Creating a Life Worth Living.* New York, HarperCollins

Maass, Donald 2002. *Writing the Breakout Novel.* Cincinnati, Writer's Digest Books

Maisel, Eric 1995. *Fearless Creating: A Step-by-Step Guide to Starting and Completing Your Work of Art.* New York, Penguin

Mamatas, Nick 2008. "Pulp Faction: Teaching 'Genre Fiction' in the Academy," *The Writer's Chronicle*, November/December, 76–89

Mayers, Timothy 2009. "One Simple Word: From Creative Writing to Creative Writing Studies," *College English*, 71:3

— 2010. "Poetry, F(r)iction, Drama: The Complex Dynamics of Audience in the Writing Workshop," in *Does the Writing Workshop Still Work?* Dianne Donnelly, ed. Clevedon, Multilingual Matters, 94–104

— 2005. *(Re)Writing Craft: Composition, Creative Writing, and the Future of English Studies.* Pittsburgh, University of Pittsburgh

McGurl, Mark 2009. *The Program Era: Postwar Fiction and the Rise of Creative Writing.* Cambridge MA, Harvard University Press

McNair, Dave 2008. "Remembering George Garrett: Uncle and Maestro," http://www.readthehook.com/stories/2008/10/02/COVER-garrettAmalg.aspx, accessed April 9 2010

Miller, Richard 2008. "The Future is Now: Presentation to the Rutgers Board of Governors" (video), http://www.youtube.com/watch?v=z65V2yKOXxM, accessed April 10 2010. Statement at 1:45

Moat, John 2005. *The Founding of Arvon: A Memoir of the Early Years of the Arvon Foundation.* London, Frances Lincoln

Moxley, Joseph 1989. *Creative Writing in America: Theory and Pedagogy.* Urbana, NCTE

Murphy Moo, Jessica 2007. "Writers In Training": Interview with Edward Delaney. http://www.theatlantic.com/magazine/archive/2007/07/writers-in-training/6077/4, accessed March 14 2010

Myers, D.G. 2006. *The Elephants Teach: Creative Writing Since 1880.* University of Chicago Press

National Association of Writers in Education 2010. "Writing Courses," http://www.nawe.co.uk/metadot/index.pl?id=2389&isa=Category&op=show, accessed March 14 2010

National Committee of Inquiry into Higher Education 1996. "The Dearing Report," http://www.leeds.ac.uk/educol/ncihe/, accessed February 18 2010

National Endowment for the Arts 2007. "Executive Summary", *To Read or Not to Read: A Question of National Consequence.* http://www.nea.gov/research/ToRead_ExecSum.pdf, accessed May 26 2010

National Literacy Trust 2010. "Literacy: State of the Nation" http://www.literacytrust.org.uk/assets/0000/3816/FINAL_Literacy_State_of_the_Nation_-_30_March_2010.pdf, accessed June 2 2010

Ostrom, Hans. Email to author, April 14 2010.

Pink, Daniel 2006. *A Whole New Mind: Why Right Brainers Will Rule the Future.* New York, Riverhead

Pipher, Mary 2006. *Writing to Change the World.* New York, Penguin

Poniwozik, James 2005. "Dave Eggers: A Literary Rebel with Causes," www.time.com/time/subscriber/2005/time100/artists/100eggers.html, accessed May 25 2010

Ritter, Kelly 2001. "Professional Writers/Writing Professionals: Revamping Teacher Training in Creative Writing Ph.D. Programs," *College English* 64:2, 205–227

Ritter, Kelly and Stephanie Vanderslice, eds. 2007. *Can It Really Be Taught?: Resisting Lore in Creative Writing Pedagogy*. Portsmouth NH, Heinemann Boynton/Cook

Roe, Sue 2010. "Introducing Masterclasses," in *Does the Writing Workshop Still Work?* Dianne Donnelly, ed. Clevedon, Multilingual Matters, 194–205

Royster, Brent 2005. "Inspiration, Creativity and Crisis: The Romantic Myth of the Writer Meets the Contemporary Classroom" in *Power and Identity in the Creative Writing Classroom: The Authority Project*. Anna Leahy, ed. Clevedon, Multilingual Matters, 26–38

Saracevic, Alan T. 2008. "Reporter's Notebook: the TED Conference," http://www.826valencia.org/press, March 11 2008. Accessed May 25, 2010

Shapiro, Karl 1992. *The Old Horsefly*. Orono ME, Northern Lights

Spandel, Vickie 2005. *The Nine Rights of Every Writer*. Portsmouth NH, Heinemann Boynton/Cook

Starkey, David and Wendy Bishop 2006. *Keywords in Creative Writing*. Logan, University of Utah

Starkey, David 2010. "The Creative Writing Workshop in the Two-Year College: Who Cares?" in *Does the Writing Workshop Still Work?* Dianne Donnelly, ed. Clevedon, Multilingual Matters, 94–104

— ed. 1998. *Teaching Writing Creatively*. Portsmouth NH, Boynton/Cook

Sutton, Keith "Catfish" 2008. "A Writer's Life," http://catfishgumbo.blogspot.com/2008/03/writers-life.html, accessed June 2 2010

Swander, Mary 2005. "Duck Duck Turkey: Using Encouragement to Structure Writing Assignments" in *Power and Identity in the Creative Writing Classroom: The Authority Project*. Anna Leahy, ed. Clevedon, Multilingual Matters, 167–179

Thebo, Mimi. Email to author. January 10 2008

Uppal, Priscila 2007 "Both Sides of the Desk: Experiencing Creative Writing Lore as a Student and as a Professor," in *Can It Really Be Taught?: Resisting Lore in Creative Writing Pedagogy*. Portsmouth NH, Heinemann Boynton/Cook

Vanderslice, Stephanie 2009. "Live From Chicago: AWP 2009 Day 2," http://wordamour.wordpress.com /2009/02/14/live-from-chicago-awp-2009-day-2/, accessed May 30 2010

—and Kelly Ritter, forthcoming. *Teaching Creative Writing to Undergraduates: A Practical Sourcebook*. Southlake TX, Fountainhead Press

Wandor, Michelene 2008. *The Author is Not Dead, Merely Somewhere Else: Creative Writing After Theory*. London, Palgrave Macmillan

Weaver, Rheyanne 2009. "Piper Writers House: Little Cottage, Big History." http://statepressmagazine.com accessed May 28, 2010

Index